Mesmerizing Poe

Rick Hammer

Based on The Mystery of Marie Rogêt

By Edgar Allan Poe

ISBN-10: 1511475471
ISBN-13: 978-1511475471

DEDICATION

For Brit

CONTENTS

ACKNOWLEDGMENTS

June 18, 1982, while my wife Brit was modeling through Elite agency in New York, another *charmeuse* she knew named Marie Josée Saint-Antoine was discovered stabbed to death. Models work wonders, not just as *femme fatales*, alluring the public eye, not just as *risqué caprices*. Yet when the latest sensation's mesmeric life was cut short, she fell victim to those who confuse enchantment with provocation. After sharing Brit's shock and horror and worry for her safety due to their likeness, we recognized the resemblance of her confidante's name to that of the murdered girl in the Poe story. Strange coincidences, that these two events happened near the same place, that each could have involved suspects who were eminent, yet indiscreet men who betrayed girls' trust. First pursuing the angle with scrutiny for the weekly newspaper *New York Press* edited by Russ Smith, illustrated by Tom Chalkley, I later developed the idea as a screenplay and a novella. Morgan Library, Paris, Philadelphia and Baltimore were resources.

Rick Hammer, March 16, 2015, Tulsa, Oklahoma.

MESMERIZING POE

1 MARY ROGERS MEETS JOHN ANDERSON

INSIDE PHOEBE Rogers's boarding house at 126 Nassau Street, in New York, on February 13, 1837, seventeen-year-old Mary Rogers and her mother rolled cigars, earnestly at the labor-intensive piecework that they had taken into their home.

This job of work was a step up from the lives of those who were rioting in the streets because they were too poor to bear the higher cost of flour. As the leatherheads dragged one away, Mary Rogers thought, sow the wind and reap the whirlwind, though grant him eternal rest as a token of remembrance. If someone could have seen beforehand what would come when President Andrew Jackson demanded payment in coin and then the price of cotton fell 25 percent, who knows if the banks will fail and joblessness will starve us all?

"Much obliged!" Mary Rogers furiously nagged her mother with a rolled newspaper. Then, she looked down thoughtfully as her volatile, fiery temperament shifted moods dramatically along with her thoughts. "... To you," she said. Her tone shifted from impetuous to annoyed. "And then much obliged to a husband. Why not to the boss? I could manage his shop."

John Anderson approached the Rogers' home strategically from the street, avoiding mud splatters. The bearded, 25-year-old, stern, rigidly honest, sole proprietor of his tobacco shop, selling cigars and Solace, the well known fine-cut chewing tobacco wrapped in foil, had come to check on his employees' drudgework. He overheard Phoebe Rogers and Mary Rogers inside, and he approached their window. He stood back in the shadows peering in through the shutters but within earshot, eaves-dropping.

Anderson could hear that Mary Rogers, out of the public eye, was drowning in her low status. She defended herself against being ground under the crowd by her urbane, articulate sarcasm. She was, after all, a New Yorker who liked to take stock of a situation with a sweeping glance. Anderson saw a blaze of debonair, alert intelligence in her glittering eyes. He liked her sweeping glances. He liked her drab expression as she listened to her mother's scolding. Anderson imagined her out of her clothes, gyrating with a dancer's sensuality, and lightness. She looked right toward him, but her eyes saw only her own reflection in the window. He saw a gesture she made as she finished a cigar and brushed the surface, a gesture that struck him in the heart: willowy and fox-like.

Anderson felt mature now, but he demanded respect for that, because he had converted his financial success to buying land in Manhattan. He had achieved his goal of providing chewing tobacco and snuff wrapped in foil to the military and distributing them, but he did not want to be pegged as a cigar-store owner. He wanted to be mayor of New York. He was handsome, bearded, thin and strong and stern. He knew business but he loved better the thrill of gambling for high stakes. He was challenging and cruel and he would love luring Mary Rogers into his web by passionate leverage. His hands struck together, knife-like, invincible.

"A smoke shop is no place for a beautiful young girl," Phoebe Rogers said.

Anderson heard a newspaper rip, and his eyes followed the two female silhouettes. The first, with a soft, sighing laugh, roused a harmonious laugh in the other.

"Principles," Mary Rogers said. "I want passion. I want sensations. I want to stir up this world."

"Your father always said: seek out the risk you are ready to whip," Phoebe Rogers said. Then she turned and pointed due north. "319 Broadway and Thompson are just around the corner from us."

"I will take Mr. John Anderson by force," Mary Rogers said. She cradled her mother.

Anderson saw Mary Rogers' shadow on the window-blind.

"...Or persuasion," Mary Rogers said. She discarded the paper.

"I'm sure you'll be prudent around dangerous friends," Phoebe Rogers said sarcastically, as they continued working. Distant piano keys played "Carnaval" by Robert Schumann.

"All men are red in tooth and claw," Phoebe Rogers

advised her daughter.

John Anderson overheard her and smiled, scheming his next move in ominous silence, and then knocked at the front door.

Phoebe Rogers opened the door. Anderson stepped in, kneeled devoutly and picked up the scrap of paper that Phoebe Rogers had dropped. Anderson turned to the sunlight and read the ad: New York Herald, John Anderson, Solace Tobacco.

"Morning," Anderson said brusquely. He returned the ad playfully to Mary Rogers. Phoebe Rogers was flustered.

"I came to check your piece-work," Anderson said to Mary Rogers. "What is your name again?"

"Mary Cecilia Rogers," she said. She freed her cheap light gray wool dress, showing off underneath her dress, her pretty 17-year-old girl's legs. She offered her hand. "The best roller of cigars in Manhattan."

Phoebe hovered protectively around Mary.

"You know I am John Anderson, maker of Solace Tobacco," he said, kissing her hand. Phoebe Rogers disapprovingly kicked tobacco shavings and picking up a broom, began tidying up the dust underfoot. Phoebe Rogers brushed the dust off the windows, light streams in through clouds of dust motes. She swept, propped open the door, and the scent floated up from the box.

"Every boy and girl in the Union wants one," Mary Rogers said, picking up a cigar.

"Your father, God rests his bones," Phoebe Rogers said, correcting Mary's behavior under her breath.

Mary Rogers then took charge of straightening the cigars in boxes for transport.

"Would you consider hiring a woman to work in your smoke shop?" Mary Rogers said, tugging at the feminine red ribbon at her neck.

"I am begging your pardon, sir," Phoebe Rogers said. She puckered and swiveled away, standing up the broom.

"Buying or selling?" Anderson said to Mary Rogers.

"By your leave, whatever you desire," Mary Rogers said.

Anderson chuckled.

"Working class girls," he whispered to himself.

Mary Rogers then approached Anderson and gave him one of the cigars she had rolled.

"You know, I saw two businessmen talking outside your shop the other day," Mary Rogers said.

"About what? Anderson asked.

"Setting up their own shop on Lower Broadway. But they were not sure if they could keep some hogsheads fresh," Mary Rogers said.

As Anderson watched Mary Rogers diplomatically, he saw through her willowy surface, and felt her subtle manipulation.

"They will soon be my competitors," Anderson said.

Anderson took Phoebe Rogers's hand in his left and Mary Rogers's hand in his right.

"I want you to come to work on Monday," Anderson said to Mary Rogers. "As shop assistant," he added, reassuringly to Phoebe Rogers. Then Anderson whispered gently, to Mary

Rogers. "You report to me. Everything."

Phoebe Rogers warily searched in her daughter's eyes for her deeper motives while nodding yes. Then Anderson started to exit, with the rolled cigars under his arm.

"Mr. Anderson reminds me so much of your father," Phoebe Rogers whispered to Mary Rogers.

"Maybe this one won't go out with the tide," Mary Rogers said. Then as Anderson exited, Mary Rogers raced after him, taking the cigars from him. "I will start right now," Mary Rogers said.

Phoebe Rogers saw Mary Rogers glance back at her with a wink, then continuing down the street with Anderson.

"And remain immune to seduction," Phoebe Rogers said to herself as if she were speaking to her daughter.

2 POE SEES MARY ROGERS

EDGAR ALLAN POE had been cast naked upon the naked earth January 19, 1809. His parents' play of passion as an actor and an actress, two performers in a traveling show business company was death defying. Although, when his parents died within a few days of each other in December 1811, he was adopted and renamed by his stepfather Edgar Allan, and then on January 7, 1812, he was baptized and christened Edgar Allan Poe.

Poe began boarding in an academy in Chelsea, within suburban London in 1816. Next he was known as Edgar Allan at the Manor House School until 1820. Returned to the United States, he eventually entered the University of Virginia in February 1826, and he was distinguished in ancient languages, although with his allowance scarce, he gambled and lost. When his stepfather refused to honor his debt, Poe sailed for Boston, where he was also known as Henri Le Rennet.

Transformed yet again in July 1830, he enlisted in the army as a cadet at West Point, where he was court-martialed and expelled for disobeying orders, February 1831. Then he eventually landed in Baltimore with his paternal aunt Maria Clemm and tutored her eight-year-old daughter Virginia. After that, the rover, foreshadowed by auguries of anger throughout his combative career, became recognized as the writer, when his tale "The Visionary" appeared in 1834.

This was the year Poe found out that the United States was about to ratify its first crime compact, between New York and New Jersey, and at about the same time, he recognized that his reasoning was the proving ground. He discovered that the death of a beautiful woman was the most visionary mood *dans le monde*, and he vividly recognized that whirling a riddle *en plus* with an enchantress could intensify his recognition.

Upon this bank and shoal of time in Baltimore, Poe was hexed and alienated from his captious critics, while *The Visionary* was broadly circulated in the January 1834 issue of the journal *Godey's Lady's Book*. There was a brilliance when the eye, like a shattered mirror multiplies the images of its sorrow.

Poe would also awaken from its long slumber the periodical *Southern Literary Messenger* in Richmond, Virginia, with *The Visionary*, where Poe was the magazinist, at times staff writer and editor and critic. This was, by the way, the month when the first electrical printing press was patented in the United States.

Poe, who was recognized by some as a young genius, began quarreling about his meager salary of about $10 a week and his liberty to write more like the first installment of *The Narrative of Arthur Gordon Pym*, then retired from editing the *Southern Literary Messenger* in Richmond, Virginia January 3, 1837, and he raced headlong with his wife and cousin, 14-year-old Virginia and his aunt Maria Clemm and their tortoise-shell tabby Catterina to New York, but he couldn't find an editorial station. Poe took up residence in February 1837 at Waverly Place and Sixth Avenue in New York. Moving into this dwelling meant sharing a floor, (partitioned off) and a table with the bookseller William Gowans. Mrs. Clemm managed a boarding house to make do.

Poe heard a haunting grandfather clock's resonant chimes as they reverberated. All ears, he made out, echoing the clock, the pilot of the Barclay Street ferry, as he clanged his mournful bell 4 times like thunderclaps from his perch at the bridge. The cranky, churning steam-driven Barclay Street ferry haggled the hard mile east across the Hudson River toward Manhattan. The ferry sliced and bucked through the fresh-water current of the Hudson River (rolling down from the north), and strained to cross against the rising whitecaps and spray of the rumbling and whirling salt-water tide of the Atlantic Ocean feeding into the Bay to the south where the eerie, obsessive, haunting bells of a buoy rocked and clanged. The ferociously glaring rising sun suddenly silhouetted its skeletal form. Overshadowing the rich warmth of the sun, the ominous pealing of thunder bounced off menacing, brooding black and blue storm clouds. Eight bells rang on the brig docked at the harbor, signaling to the sailors forenoon watch. They craned their necks as they peered uneasily overhead to rocking masts and whipping sails and flailing riggings auguring the squall rushing in from the Nor-theast. On the New Jersey shore, a passenger train rushed by groaning trees as the engineer signaled one long and one short: t-o-o-t, toot.

Above Poe walked Mary Rogers and her mother Phoebe, as they cut through the traffic.

"Here is a deeper muse," Poe said. He spoke for the benefit of a newsboy named Tibbs. Then Poe stood up, attracted to the stranger passing in the crowd. He saw her spin around, see Poe and then look away, without recognition.

Tibbs punched Poe. Poe's words were trampled by the clopping hooves of dray horses as their legs strained against clanging riggings, pulling a cart stacked with flayed skins.

Poe looked down at his cards and strategized.

Crunch. Slam. The coal vendor jammed his shovel in a staved barrel of charcoal which read: Peach Orchard Red Ash Coal, screened, broken or egg, $8 per chaldron, Jas. Ferguson.

Bang! The cards flew, money spilled, and stumps were knocked over as bundles of New York Heralds were slammed down for delivery.

"Hurry up and procrastinate," Tibbs grumbled. The newsboys pocketed their winnings and quit their game. Poe started walking home.

"Extra!" The newsboys cried, as they cut the binding strings and began hawking their papers.

Click! Click! Click! The shellfish shucker slipped his blade under the mantle edge and flipped out the saddle rock oyster and pitched the shell onto a mountain of blue points wheeled in by cart and braked against the curb. The melted ice fell from the cart, drip, drip, and drip.

"Resurrectionists peddle dead bodies!" Tibbs read the headline with pretended shock.

The faces of the passersby wheeled around to confront the morbid, mock-excitable newsboys. Then one jaded New Yorker shrugged and bought a paper and hurried on to work.

"Body snatchers," Poe muttered to himself.

Poe could see Mary Rogers as she shuddered at the words, and slipped on a cobblestone but recovered her balance, and turned away, waving with disdain. And then Mary and Phoebe Rogers vanished into the shadows.

The butcher in his stall banged down his blade: chunk! Chunk! Chunk! He stood at his stall, chopping red tissue down to the bone. Then zing! He honed his blade on carborundum, and then shielded his eyes from the glaring sun. Whack! Whack! Whack! "Hot enough to roast an ox!" the butcher said to Poe.

Whing! Whing! Whing! The razor strop man whisked a straightedge, while heaving a wicker basket of wares.

Poe strutted across the shadow of a wrought iron fence that jutted up like a row of shucker's knives.

Poe could hear Liszt's "Après Une Lecture de Dante" from the distant piano now. The tender tone poem climbed and then exploded into fierce cascades in an augmented fourth. The furious chromatic scale echoed Poe's favorite obsessions, the secrets of life and death, as he exited the street, arriving at Mrs. Clemm's boarding house on Carmine Street.

Poe had a vague, yet thrilling half-credence in the supernatural, the shadow and the spirituality. He could calculate the coincidental and also the probable. Yet, he when he first saw Mary Rogers, he followed her and so discovered that she was working at Mr. Anderson's palatial Solace cigar and tobacco shop on Pine Street and Broadway, where Poe hobnobbed with a handful of authors, including Washington Irving, he was also mesmerized by the ethereal enchantress and fell under the muse's spell. Poe began writing in his imagination an *étude* about her and her powerful lover Anderson, whom he overheard describing how they had been evading the city routine to escape for a *genre* of second nature, in a wild, forested sphere across the river in Elysian Fields. Within these natural *alentours*, their passionate rapports took root. Poe in his own little *jeu de theater* played out how she could fall victim to an escape artist like Anderson and his schemes. For Poe, that set the stage for the story immured here, the kind of mystery that can rarely be resolved. He was swept away by her, and he would daydream in entrancement, by using his rare prescience. He would cast waves of thespian ratiocination deeply and magically shuddering from hell to breakfast, with his vital psychic force. So, throughout his fervent dream he would eavesdrop, and her terror of Anderson's anger echoed within his soul. What he overheard was poised uncannily, on the verge of his keys to kingdom come.

Writing was his duty, to fill his debt's bottomless, raging river.

Je ne sais quoi made him weather the storm by stiffening both his rye whiskey and his backbone, yet Poe, intuitive *provocateur*, acted on self-confidence and guessed ahead, and he worked his way up fast and loose, despite his rivals.

When rang the blame, that he was not as good as the visionary he was before, it struck Poe as evocative of the faults many a censure slinger could twist toward a well-made play or *la pièce bien faite*.

Portents brewed in Poe's mind that letters to come could bring a change of fortune.

Thus, if Poe had been rootless far too freely, he was crossing the threshold from the first stage of his life and into the revelations that he was about to bring through his writing.

Perhaps it felt to him as if he had been acting on a stage, even nightwalking, as a noctambulist, yet now he was seeing his future on the distant horizon, like the Fury Alecto.

If Poe's way of working was to never make the reader trust the artist, just the tale, then perhaps the revelation came to him that he could be more than himself when he pretended to be something more. In this stage, with a reversal swinging to a quick dénouement, he found by being panned that he was returned to his rightful place in the older order. In the days to come, there were many more *personae* in his repertoire.

Poe also saw the light upon the depths of his unspoken own dark mind dwelling in his Gothic imagination. So, he then cast in his own deep-toned defense mechanism an idealistic cynic's tone as The Narrator of his stories. The Narrator responded in a third person limited manner, because he knew the thoughts and feelings of Poe as the main character in this story, and so he adhered closely to his perspective as if he were Poe's looking-glass.

And so, The Narrator pitched in, together with Poe in his pitch-dark imagination, scathing poetasters with fearless opinions and the sternest sense of literary justice along with the *sobriquet* tomahawk man.

As The Narrator had worked as an oracle, he echoed Poe, who was haunted because he wanted to feel the touch of another on his skin. Poe, through these nascent ruminations endured the melancholy of his edgy, restless life, soon allotting a morbid tone to the mood of his writing.

3 POE AND *PYM*

When the first installment had been published of his singular novel, *The Narrative of Arthur Gordon Pym of Nantucket* in late January 1837 in the *Southern Literary Messenger*, some faultfinders had already castigated Poe for his rash fabrication of Pym. Notwithstanding the calcified skein doling out print back then, Poe's alter ego Pym had written that by degrees he had felt the greatest desire to go to sea in his sail-boat Ariel, on some of the maddest freaks in the world, and by now it appeared to him a thousand wonders that he was alive to-day.

And so, Poe's peripatetic doubleness appeared, even as Poe arose from his own invented *pur sang* background into his marriage with its requirement of providing his wife and *protégé* Virginia, nicknamed Sissy, his quiet attentions. Poe and Sissy found between their mingling and their opposition, the mysterious vibrations of kindred tones. Consequently, from first to last in his writing, his passions and principles that were once steady in their frenzy began to shift and waver even as he returned to reason.

"It is madness to make fortune the mistress of events. My destiny hangs by a thread, Sissy," Poe said.

"Mind your tempering with realism," Sissy said.

Poe called her Sissy or Sis and he was obliged to coddle her through all this, since she was his childlike first cousin Virginia Clemm, with whom he had signed a marriage bond on May 16, 1836, while she was 13, a liaison some say was like brother and sister, perhaps because of her nickname. Yet, Poe also tolerated a more shrouded spirit hovering always within earshot, Virginia's mother, Maria, who glimpsed each time he budged. His nickname for her was Muddie.

Poe scribbled an idea for *Ligeia*, a story that might be interpreted as a hallucination told by The Narrator, who is an opium addict, about a raven-haired beauty with knowledge of forbidden wisdom, who dies and then is revived, perhaps by witchcraft. *Saducismus Triumphatus* had affirmed the aspersive supernatural powers of witches.

When Poe heard the critics murmur that he was obsessed with life beyond death, he took a moment, and he spoke in dark juxtaposition to his alter ego, the Narrator, whom he had written in as the mirror of his soul, sonorous as a double face of expression and illusion.

"I echo your loneliness, beneath your cloak of secrecy, *entourée de mystère*," the Narrator said.

"My thirst might scarcely be endured," Poe said. "I try to relieve it by wine, fighting fire with fire. That has excited me to a high degree of intoxication, for another sleepless night."

Poe heard suddenly stirring the agonizing extremity of racket a little before daybreak. Gazing at his reflection in the window across from the printers, toward the stoop where he was hunched, with the front page of the magazine nailed to the board above his head, he gazed at the unquiet pallor of his own countenance staring back at his gaze, falling in love with his sad reflection.

"You are the genius of this scene," the Narrator said.

"Even with the gaze of the departed still fixed upon me?" Poe said. "I have felt so awkward when left alone, that the windowpane makes in my image a mannikin, merely to madden me."

"Yet, you have sensed within your spirit, your own pathway through the course of mystery and occultism and the cunning, lurid stars," the Narrator said.

"I have mastered my way sometimes, through fluency in French," Poe said. "Yet my mesmeric revelation is lost by seasoned, impulsive gambling and its haunting debts."

"Drinking whiskey, wine, port and rummy coffee is a course you may have followed through unknown channels," the Narrator said.

"Although my poetic gift flows in its restless fine frenzy," Poe said.

"You could say its doubling looks back at you like your twist of fate," the Narrator said.

"Since you who read are still among the living, this year has been a year of terror," Poe said. "Still, when I who write shall have long since gone my way into the region of shadows, secret things shall be known."

"My feelings are more intense than terror," the Narrator said.

"And the heaviness in the atmosphere around us is a dead weight hung upon me for which there is no name upon the earth except psychal impressions of anxiety," Poe said.

"Even if Psyche is the ambiguous voice of your conscience?" the Narrator said.

"Even if I am a pale poet, who believes that every poem should not preach a moral, " Poe said.

"Your eyes are gray, and there is a darkness within them some recognize as singular," the Narrator said.

"What's more, the long shadow of my character is cast through a glass, darkly, while I am tranced in silence," Poe said.

"Despite the isolation of your soul's secret *mêlée*, you are just getting by as a journeyman editor, known for fixing other writer's clumsy turns of phrase," the Narrator said.

"Yet, in the days to come, because I am also a hustling, cocky, clever underdog reporter, I could stumble through the vulgar froth and scum of my line of work," Poe said.

"Diving, keenly addicted, into the dramatic strokes of sensationalism," the Narrator said.

"Not to fade away, a shadow such as the moon, when low in heaven, might fashion from my figure, vague and formless," Poe said. "I will cast down my eyes, with the tones in my voice not just the shade of any one being, but of a multitude of beings, varying in their cadences from syllable to syllable, falling duskly upon my ears in the well-remembered and familiar accents of many thousand departed friends.

Tantalizing unsolved opportunities compelled acute minds like Edgar Allan Poe's to probe. The enigma Poe faced, that he wanted to echo his childhood hero Lord Byron and seize the fascination of the public, was vivid. Poe was aroused and frequently fascinated by true crime. He sometimes felt he had a sixth sense, so that he could actually solve the crime. Right along with them, Poe would cast himself as the interrogator, then Poe became the seeker after evidence, who through his combative intelligence and his will power, searched for what could be found despite any presentiment of death. The riddle of a lost girl's whereabouts could, therefore become heightened because she was the most coveted. The obscure object of desire was most thrilling while the most at risk, through warnings and portents and evils imminent. For Poe, moreover, there was his double consciousness, his twilight states of somnambulism, and his cryptomnesia, that he used to help solve popular crimes, forerunners of those who would study psychology and the occult. To place this sort of mystery in context, Poe was intrigued as were many. If a name was recognized or if a location was well known, or if she had also relaxed in a prominent location for leisure entertainment by many people, then Poe built a moral bridge in his imagination, to where she went missing. Poe's methods of problem solving were better than those common in the popular media of the time, and more straightforward and more useful and more honest.

Perhaps Poe himself tasted the drug of deception and plunged into tragedy, because he was the tormented amateur analyst while he was on the trail of a real killer. In 1837 that might have seemed *outré*, yet today it seems orthodox. Then Poe's singular style required a first-hand balance to tell a story so startling.

Poe used the tools of his trade to solve a mystery, his obsession with the undercurrent of intrigue in the privileged class, his devilish audacity to discover power's inner secrets and the mooring of his own ferocious addiction to drinking.

The extent of the information obtained lies not so much in the validity of the inference as in the quality of the observation.

The best cautionary tale of mystery and suspense shows the actual historical reporting covered by Poe while he was reading published newspaper accounts. He started to imagine a character he could play, a voice that could speak his insights into cracking crimes. This could mean solving the homicide of a beautiful young girl. There could be subterfuge, and a suspenseful moment when the most felon winds cleared the guilty of all suspicion. Sardonically foreshadowing what was to come, the private investigations of Poe worked best while he converted the story telling to the voice of his alter ego, *le chevalier sans peur et sans reproche*, (the knight without fear and beyond reproach) in the Légion d'honneur, Le Chevalier César Auguste Dupin. This likeness to Poe in exile shows how his far-ranging erudition fit its frame. His unnamed stream-of-consciousness Narrator served his master faithfully.

In a surprising and unsettling way, Poe would write in his Philosophy of Composition, "The death, then, of a beautiful woman is, unquestionably the most poetical topic in the world..." Ultimately, while arousing the fascination of the public, some say Poe's persona Dupin masked the darker Gothic depths of his bipolar disorder.

The character called the Narrator served to mystify Poe's stream of consciousness through evoking remembrances of things past. So, the Narrator also revealed involuntary recurrent memories of past events for the reader. While telling a story within a story, Poe's observations showed him, as you will see, working as if in real time, discovering the killer's opportunity, his method and his motive.

4 POE INVOKES HIS MUSE

POE WALKED downstairs and saw Muddie and Sissy's breakfasts lying on the dining room table: creamed herring with goat cheese and hardtack and then a balance book against a stack of unpaid bills and a chewed pencil and a worn-out checkbook. Poe opened the door and saw what looked like a cloud in the background. He walked through the door as if through a scrim. And then he was standing in a mist. The oak branches shivered in the wind. The birds were calling out low and close due to the weather. First were a grackle's call and then a blue jay's call and then a mockingbird's call. Poe made out the sound of the train shuffling by and blowing its whistle and passing by.

Poe smelled the rot of the old wood patched together out of rough split hemlock timbers strung with rope and he heard the rattle of the galvanized tin and felt the breeze through the cracks in the wall.

Poe was a visionary and dreamy but his mind was bending into a new form. Muddie brought out his breakfast: a serving of broiled beef brisket broiled, and black coffee and scrambled eggs and smoke. On that wall behind was a sketch he had scrawled in charcoal: a masked angel climbing upstairs through swirling tornadoes of smoke roiling over a wild forest of beasts and horned devils who brandished arrows spears and swords.

Poe had tacked a draft of his outline on the wall as proof of his progress. He could tell he was coming unhinged, and was stuck with his obsessions as they were. His only hope was transforming his obsessions into new forms. But at the heart of it his obsessions were the same. With the boarders around, he did not feel so cloistered as he had when he was alone and expecting no one.

He gazed out over the backdrop of a garden that had been weeded and a birch that seemed to be waiting for spring.

Poe could see Mary Rogers there, arising magically. Her hair had grown down to her shoulders. Poe could only see Mary Rogers through a glass darkly. The boarding house was lit dimly from the overcast sky. Muddie had left on the table a long-stemmed wine glass of white Bor-deaux that quivered and swelled anamorphically when anyone walked by. Poe looked at the reflection like a voyeur. What about a writer who stayed behind writing like a shadow of his great characters?

Poe could see on the opposite corner an old three-story manor house where a workman was shoring up the ruins. The weathered red brick, structure was almost excluded from passers-by; bushes and a three-foot tall wall shielded it. Tendrils of brown winter-dried and brittle ivy squirmed over its surface. The house had been built on a grand scale, with three stories and on the roof skylights peeking out from French chimneys. The walls were brick but there were Doric capstones that helped present the illusion of columns. I chose this shell because my mind is also in need of repair, with my restless sleep, my recurring nightmare, my poorly masked anxiety. He bet now with moist palms and tense posture and a strained voice. He heard his words, pressured and hesitant and intensely emotional. Only under the most stressful circumstances would Poe display his feelings of detachment from himself or his environment. Poe knew he was writing this to clear his mind of her forever.

"Come closer so I can see you better," Poe said.

"Distance lends enchantment," Mary Rogers said.

"I will never do anything to hurt you," Poe said.

"I want to talk about us," Mary Rogers said. "Do you care about me at all?"

"All I can do is write," Poe said. "I am not your shill. I have too much at stake."

"How do you think I feel having somebody put words into my mouth?" Mary Rogers asked. "It was my heart that got broken."

"I have to write this my way," Poe said.

"I am outside your ways. The dead are the only ones outside the law," Mary Rogers said.

"I am just a journey-man writer," Poe said. "I rattle away at my day-job so I can write at night. I am intense and moody and lucid at times and at other times bull-headed and vain. I need you because I am fascinated by your story."

"You think I am perfectly unattainable," Mary Rogers said.

"You are fixated on me."

"You haunt me," Poe said. "I feel like I am living with a veiled allusion." Then Muddie and Sissie came in and Poe disregarded what he could see of Mary Rogers in the corner of his eye.

Poe would retreat back to his sternway, where he could work alone in his sultry cell. Poe could let down his mask there, the mask intended to hide the fact that he was a dreamy, flawed visionary, who idolized beauty. Flawed because his writing had released from inside his spirit something morbid and bizarre. His terror of his mercurial drinking and gambling had driven him down into this rut. And now Mary Rogers, once his fantasy and now his ghost was threatening to pull him out of the shadows and out into the light.

Dream friction started under the covers while Poe was still sleeping. Poe felt the tide rocking him. Then he felt Mary Rogers straightening her nightgown. She began negotiating his body with her curious hands. He felt the tips of her fingers extending and then escaping, bird-like. Poe squirmed sleepily.

Poe dominated Mary Rogers's frame with his arm, driving her down into the bed until she surrendered and was powerless to resist him. This was the heart of her seduction. The trees outside rustled in counterpoint, teasing with their dry rattling brushes. Poe drove himself inside and then pulled back again and again. Poe left her frame tense as he straddled her. Poe felt his anger rushing stiffly through him. Mary Rogers was lying still, but unwilling. Then mercurially, she consented. Poe rocked his leg between her legs. She resisted. Poe's pen stood overlooking her lips, which broke into a channel in the wake of her rooster-tail of light brunette pubic hair and he crossed her wake. Then Mary Rogers felt pushed, not romanced and would not. Poe knelt in front of her, gnarling his muscles and reaching down and kneading between her thighs. Mary Rogers started to laugh and forced Poe down on his knees.

Poe drove into her and she was wet, but then she wrestled free and sat up quickly against the bedstead. Poe sat up, his pen arching like a raven, waiting to clamber over her. Poe rolled over and forced his eyes shut, seeing in the dark a red trail of sparks vanishing and in the corner of one eye a moon coming up after Venus and then he rolled over. A long stretch of silence and the loneliness between them stretched like a divide.

Poe took out a bottle of sherry and gave himself a sip. Then Poe sank back against the buckled sheets, bobbing. Mary Rogers crawled on top of him, with her bareness, but moist and gummy inside. She then stood up, her silhouette against the window. She looked out toward the tree that resisted the wind, blowing strong and arid and cool. Then Mary Rogers turned back toward the sheets' white-caps. Her sandy skin held the salve within. When Poe reached out for her, his root tuber was still seeking her to sleep in. She browsed over his body. Then Mary Rogers fell down next to Poe, gazing toward him sleepily. Poe pulled her body up to his. She was lithe and she was the leonine one. He peered down into her pudenda, like a fire glowing under the ash. Mary Rogers's hair swept away from him like clouds of raw smoke washing across stars. She dipped her eyes down like Draco's strand of stars diving into the bay for a lick across the water. Then she straightened up, pumping her legs and she lolled around the bed. Poe seized Mary Rogers by the frame of her shoulders and pulled her back to bed. He started to make crude love to her while gazing into her eyes with the mark of a failed artist, the searching look in his eyes.

Mary Rogers pulled Poe toward her, sleepily. He was randy and cantankerous and his manhood was tied up in knots and aching. Poe stretched out beside her wasted. She fell asleep. But then she woke up and reached for him with her lips hot. She dove for his neck with her mouth. She swam hard against him. Her legs kneaded his rocks. His branch sought her with real hunger. The hunger became contagious. He bundled her in the sheets like swaddling bedclothes and drank in her cream. Then he drove the head of his pen into her. She wanted it. She combed aside her velvety hair against the mushroom tip. Mary Rogers rolled over and pulled up one leg like a cat. Poe turns the head around and around an inch inside her. She ground to be pacified, swaying as she opened up her patch to him. She nestled his rocks in her small fingers. They were working at cross-purposes in an uneasy balance of rhythms, punishing each other and keeping on. She wanted him to keep on. She teased him with her dance. He kept on prodding her.

Mary Rogers was lost for the moment in her old daydream where she had been trapped in the snow while the train stormed by. She lay in a fur coat with the hood and he was keeping her warm and snow was jamming the tunnel like crystal of prisms and white and she was still and warm in the crotch of a tree.

Then Poe began frenching her nipples and they were soft and pliant under his tongue. Then Poe took the branch in his hand again and snuck in to the pliant small lips and she lay there running against him.

And then Poe pulled her back against the bed and he climbed onto her flinging his desire against her. Poe's fingers searched along the base of her spine for a handhold. Poe looked down the field of her body along the range of tiny blonde hairs sweeping up and rippling down with her breathing and he looked further down toward the bearded hide-away where he was headed. Then she came back and they burrowed together, her body squirming into him until both of their desires were fulfilled.

Not long after Poe's fantasy, he walked into Anderson's Solace Cigar Store. Anderson was gone, but Mary Rogers sold Poe a cigar.

"You are a dreamer," Mary Rogers said to Poe. Poe could see himself in her eyes, ruminative, melancholy and self-contemptuous and fatalistic.

"Nothing happens that has not happened before?" Poe said. ""What good is it to be a copy-cat?"

"Those are bitter words," Mary Rogers said.

"Look, the rules are different here than when I was a boy onstage," Poe said. "You can not talk morals here. There are not any true believers here."

"Are you always so certain about everything?" Mary Rogers said.

"Dead right," Poe said.

"How do I look?" Mary Rogers said. He whistled.

"The devil is in the details," Poe said.

"You have such absolute standards," Mary Rogers said.

"Do you have any desire for me? Are you one of those men who only want to make love when you want to be forgiven? Are you chasing yourself?" Poe reached out to touch Mary Rogers, but she slipped away.

"I am always looking for work," Poe said.

"You probably spend money like an alcoholic," Mary Rogers said. "You only pay the bills under the gun, right?"

"So be it," Poe said. "Some people sleep to touch something from another world."

"I sleep alone," Mary Rogers said. "I have had my tarot cards read, though I am scared of the occult, of witches and all that. I am seeking something."

Poe felt reckless and he mulled over how lost she appeared.

"You have something boiling up inside you," Poe started to point out the unusual duration of this spell until he realized the probable cause, her boss. She could see what he was thinking. "Emotional complications can lead like a bad debt, and a dun never forgives or forgets or forgoes. For nothing. But for what you owe.

And when it is time to settle up, you feel like a fool. You feel trapped, sooner or later you always do." Then Poe tried to shrug it off.

"Is this the end?" Mary Rogers said. "If I change everything about my life, would anyone really need me? What would you do if this were the end?" Poe could feel her resisting the delicate conversational thread that bound them and strained between them and was now threatening to tangle and gore them both. "We have each gone through stages. It has been day-to-day sometimes before.

"I might have a nervous breakdown," Mary Rogers said. "If I am late on a job, I explain my intentions, I ask for understanding, and ask for forgiveness for my laziness. Can I be your muse? How can I keep body and soul together? I used to think you knew everything."

As Poe struggled to understand her, anger criss-crossed his face. He was careful not to bare the razor of superiority.

"I am a moon-child. A full moon soon," Mary Rogers said. "I want to cry, but I am not going to let myself."

"I can not make you happy," Poe said. He fell back against the windowsill. "When I started the job I am doing now, I thought it would solve all my problems. But now I have got bigger ones."

"Are you the one who said everything works out for the good?" Mary Rogers said.

"I do not know," Poe said. "There are some pretty bad people in this world. I think we are all pretty bad inside, and some of us are better at covering it up." Poe lit the cigar and waited to let the smoke stand against the light.

"Premonitions come with feeling like fate," Mary Rogers said. "Maybe it was fate that we met. I imagined you before. And then when I saw you, I said: This Is Him! I had a dream last night and Satan said my life was not so bad. It did not matter if I had done bad things. I should make myself ready to die."

"That would be very inconvenient," Poe said, and he gazed out the window.

5 POE'S HEARTBREAKING STORIES

By March 1837 the *Messenger* appeared again with the second episode of *Pym*, and Poe attended the booksellers dinner, where he stood and toasted the monthlies of Gotham and their editors and another like-minded writer Washington Irving (the mood of whose stories blended harmoniously the supernatural amid the real by allusions to dreams, and who had also written that great minds rise above misfortune).

Yet, back at home Poe said, "My spirit is foreshadowed by another day of anxiety and fatigue, so I will withdraw within my dark second nature, since everything I planned for around New York seems nowhere to be found, like a pipe dream."

"You will surely reap where you have sown," Sissy said.

"*Cette histoire déchirante m'a bouleversée.* No need for my heartbreaking story to overwhelm you," Poe said.

Poe saw her telltale expression meant she knew better than anyone when he was merely teasing.

"Your face is a book where men may read strange matters," Poe said. Her enchanting smile brought comfort.

Which soon came in handy, since the bank panic of May 10, 1837 turned paper money to rubbish, and credit was refused, launching one of the worst economic downfalls in American history. Poe recognized that work was past praying for, so he moved Virginia and her mother into a dwelling at 113 1/2 Carmine Street in New York City.

Despite these frequently puzzling financial challenges, Poe the writer had no qualms that human ingenuity could not construct an enigma that he could not resolve, no matter how cryptic. So, he was before long led through thanatology to unravel mysteries.

And when Poe revealed to The Narrator that the best prophet is the one who guesses the best, he knew it foreshadowed his own preoccupation with the enticing theme of entertaining death as a friend who will open the gates of fame, and shut the gates of envy after it, so it becomes s final awakening.

Poe endured a restless night amid his social and financial upheaval, and murmured to his only friend The Narrator, (who could be weaving this tale), some quiet words about rendering the duel for domination between the reader and the author. He then fell asleep in the June haze near dawn in the street by the front door of *The American Monthly Magazine*. He was hoping to see his story *Von Jung, the Mystific* that was due to be printed in this periodical. Guessing ahead was his stock in trade, since his *état d'esprit* was noetic.

"Hey, Eddie, wake up. Solve any murder mysteries today?" Tibbs's raspy bark cut through the early morning maelstrom. "You can solve any challenge in respect to secrets, decipher even the most abstruse?" Tibbs's voice rang with the sarcastic soul of the 16-year-old cutthroat reporter-to-be and smart aleck, who was surrounded by the cronies he had been dealing cards to. The bundles of paper meant for print were the backdrop for Tibbs.

"At midnight in the month of June," Tibbs quoted Eddie's poem "The Sleeper" from 1831. "I stand beneath the mystic moon. In opiate vapor, dewy, dim, Exhales from out her golden rim…"

When Poe jerked himself awake, he recognized Tibbs and turned, while his only friend, the Narrator vanished.

"So what if the mysteries I write make my readers feel like detectives?" Poe said. "So what if I am obsessed by tales in which a fragile, delicate woman is drawn into romance, antiquity, chilling suspense and carnal terror."

Poe drew nearer as Tibbs flicked down his hand of cards and started counting up his winnings from the hemlock stump. Poe watched as the newsboys grumbled over their losses.

"Game of chance, boys?" Poe muttered, peering around the circle. "All from good families, with liberal opportunities for mental culture, but for the cankers in their hearts, their reckless pride."

Poe stood 5 feet 8 inches tall, 135 pounds, across from the wiry Tibbs and waited for an offer to join the card game. Poe was known as erratic and impulsive, with the fast-paced, dramatically entertaining but vain and rhythmical gestures of a card dealer. He had been expelled from the University of Virginia for gambling and expelled from West Point, where he was known as Edgar Perry. Poe could also adopt a high-toned British accent from his five years of education there, and he had retained the dangerous demeanor of an outcast thoroughbred, but his dialectics and mannerisms were smoothly Southern.

"What art thou dreaming here?" Tibbs said to Poe.

Poe was already known for the hypnotic gaze that locked Tibbs's eyes. In like manner, those in this neighborhood called him detached, jaded, a southerner-in-exile. But the fixed look in his eyes reflected a deeper muse. He had the superficial trappings of a poet, his hair was disheveled over his high, pronounced forehead and his proper clothes had been worn to a glossy black sheen. But his eyes strained to mask the romantic instincts, which were symbolized in his work: his alien self-consciousness, his swaggering, singular gambler's flamboyance and his moody, simmering internal passions. And yet, what the newsboys and publishers didn't know about Poe was that he had proven himself as an athlete

swimmingly, since his archetype was Lord Byron, poet who had

mastered the Hellespont.

But Poe felt right at home now with this workaday crew,

hustling cards in the open street-market, because when you're

published, you deserve some credit. And they liked him because he

made his deadlines, but with apt disdain. The newsboys respected

Poe's gifted, crude but literate tongue because in this newly in-

dustrialized world, gathering, editing and publishing the written

word could be turned into hard currency.

Tibbs sneered across to Poe, dealt a hand for him and then

waited for his bid. Plop! Sweat dripped off Poe's crimped forehead

and onto a jack of spades lying in the dirt. But then Poe's wary,

deadpan glance was interrupted by a shadow overhead. Incensed,

he raised his hand, to shield his eyes from the glare of the sun, as

he blinked to identify the interloper. A raven circled overhead and

wheeled toward the bay.

But, then, unexpectedly, Poe's blood throbbed at first sight of Mary Cecelia Rogers. He felt as if she were passing over his head, cutting through the traffic. His mercurial passion for her working-class form had stunned him, because Mary's face branded his imagination with desire. He was intrigued by the way her radiant 25-year-old girl's figure moved under her light, gray wool dress as she steadied a wicker basket of eggs. She turned, her slight reflection appearing in the recessed windows of storefronts adjoining a gin tavern. But always, right behind her had sauntered Phoebe Rogers, her 45-year-old mother, wearing powdery make-up and a dated, threadbare cast-off twilled scotch gingham dress.

Poe felt a punch in the ribs from Tibbs as within Poe's mind both Mary Rogers and her mother vanished into the shadows.

"I was admiring the necromancy of her female gracefulness," Poe said to Tibbs. The newsboys snorted, but sweltering, hiding their cards, they returned to their game.

"I hate to dissipate your delusion," Poe said, laying down his hand.

The brief mechanical strains of Hector Berlioz's "Symphonie Fantastique," played at a distant rehearsal hall but then were drowned out by the tide of myriad languages and the racket of the street-market.

A workman was driving one nail every inch into the front door, which was constructed of three layers of wood nailed together. Poe walked into his shadowy home, under 6-feet-2-inch ceilings. He faced at the entrance an open fireplace with a rotis-serie spit in the kitchen. Poe slipped through the front room, walked beside the fireplace, and opened a hidden door leading up a narrow secret passageway. The staircase, which was three feet wide, led to a secret garret bedroom under the gable. In the bedroom stood a short bed, a small table with a glass whale oil lamp and a chair.

Mrs. Clemm came upstairs to clean and was stunned to see Poe's shadow shaving at a 2-by-3 foot mirror framed in wood, on a table standing by a bowl of water. He was startled to see her flurrying frame and he nicked his chin.

"Hello Muddie," Poe said to Mrs. Clemm, his mother-in-law.

"Eddie!" Mrs. Clemm said. "I do not understand why we have to stay in Manhattan."

"In Manhattan a writer is surrounded by publishers," Poe said. He wiped off the shaving foam and stanched the bleeding from the razor nick on his chin. "...And competitors," Poe muttered. He watched himself in the mirror. The clock chimed. "And deadlines." Poe washed his face for and changed his shirt.

Poe and Mrs. Clemm then walked downstairs together.

"Morning, Sissy," Poe said. Virginia Eliza Clemm, Poe's wife and cousin, aged 19, huddled next to her mother. She searched Poe's face for approval, since he was her tutor and husband. Her stunning eyes were expressive, poignant and intelligent. Her fingers flipped the well-read pages of his copy of Anatomy of Melancholy.

"Eddie? What does this mean: Es giebt eine Reihe idealischer Begebenheiten, die der Wirklichkeit parallel lauft?" Sissy asked.

"We all have to work for a living," Muddie said.

"Your mother believes writing is for dreamers," Poe explained. "There are ideal series of events which run parallel with the real ones. They rarely coincide. Men and circumstances generally modify the ideal train of events, so that it seems imperfect, and its consequences are equally imperfect. Novalis wrote that.

"Did your syrupy words pay" Mrs. Clemm said gruffly. Then she stopped herself. She watched his silhouette move through shadows and light, about to take flight, raven-like.

"...Last month's rent?" Poe said. His tone was mocking. "I'll be bringing it home with me, or my name isn't..." he said mimicking an Irish brogue.

Muddie muttered and she slammed the door.

Poe recoiled, fitting his disheartened and bitter spirit.

"Eddie. The man in the middle," Sissy said. She offered Poe a drink. "Tough like a man, as touchy as a woman."

The grandfather clock chimed once, hollowly and alone.

"Why can you not bring in more money, Eddie?" Mrs. Clemm said.

"If I can publicize my role in the literary world, then the money should follow," Poe explained. Poe relapsed into his old habits of moody reverie. He was prone to abstraction and he readily assumed this shadowy state of mind with the ease of putting on a mask. "I have sometimes thrown the future to the winds and dozed off in the present, weaving the dull world around us into dreams," Poe said.

"What about real work?" Mrs. Clemm said.

"I am a calm thinker but I have been startled by coincidences into a vague, yet thrilling half-credence in the supernatural," Poe said. "This half-credence doesn't even have the full force of thought but is more chance or speculation than good judgment. But scientific methods of skeptical inquiry can be applied to the shadows of spiritual speculation."

Mrs. Clemm turned away from him then, frustrated and perplexed.

"Coincidences?" Mrs. Clemm said. "I don't understand your solution to murders."

"Never mind," Poe said. He escaped reluctantly to his room to gather up his papers. He hushed at his work, crouched at his pens and papers like a human question mark. Sultry August. Unforgiving humidity. The jangled barb of his obligations again. Muddy, the buzzing wasp in his unction, kept on droning. Then Sissy's tiny fist started tapping. Poe tilted against the near side of the door with his stern but cool surface that masked his troubles. He was a dreamy flawed visionary who idolized beauty. Flawed because he had gambled everything and when he had lost, the chaos released from inside his spirit something morbid and bizarre. His own terror had trudged him down into the rut of journeyman editor. Poe masked his troubles behind a dead pan, but underneath skulked a grisly heart.

"Eddie?" Sissy asked.

"What?" Poe rumbled. Brush the stinger away. But suddenly with the sound of her voice everything changed. The voice called from the dark side of the moon, its startling undertow drew him back into a cavernous wave of intuition meaning: what was and what will be are in motion. Poe peeked around the door and saw again a vision unveiled from his fantasies, an image of rare beauty, simple and elegant, with the fluid spring of a cat, so that the glow in her face was lunar. And that was just what Poe could see of her.

Poe took her in his arms. She needed reassurance he was there sometimes, especially while they climbing out of the dead zone of night. She sounded fresh now, and looked unvarnished and plain. Her skin was glazed with stark white, but the texture was sweet and soft like kid gloves. Her skin was flawless but gessoed and bony. Poe looked at her angel's face and then he could never look away. Her head was a little sea-bird's. Her eyes were molded and sculpted with ideal, sorrowful and intense eyelids. And when she began to talk the unexpected touch was her personality, which was well-spoken but a little shy and unsure with strangers, as though she had never been given any credence or listened to. "Let us have some fun later when I get home," Poe said. "I am always crossing thresholds, and stirring up a little trouble. I was not put on this earth for any other high and mighty reason."

"Do not talk about serious things, Eddie," Sissy said. Poe was struggling to lift her up above the worries and fears and concerns of poor people. But even though he loved this child, in form such a perfect matrix, he seemed to be racing away from her all the time. Poe paced across the room, trying to settle his muddled thoughts and make harmony out of them.

"Hey, wait a minute, where are you going? Don't leave," Sissy said. Poe did not realize until he heard himself give in that he was being seduced. Sissy led him into his writing studio.

Distance lends enchantment, Poe thought. He contemplated her face and then, suddenly, noticed its likeness to another. The face had not changed, and yet he saw it differently. For Poe, Sissy's voice recalled another person's voice, his mother's maybe, but she had died when he was a child. Poe had to concentrate on his image of her face to keep her straight. From the first, his experience of Sissy was not a simple reaction, but a mixing of memory and sensation which seized and shaped her with another's transposed parts: he had built more into her with the memory of this other shadow-person than he took out by his perception. This unfortunate circumstance left Poe in a quandary, as if his attention were divided by not-quite-simultaneous strikes of tonic and subdominant chords on a piano. It was the differences that made his aware of people's qualities at all. But when he saw similarities between himself and Sissy, he felt weak, as if his own motives were hidden from him. It have been that the reason given to others were invented after the inherently ambivalent fact, and composed to cover up a blind impulse, as the curtain to eclipse some necessarily fine and private place. But because of Muddie, any burning passion that spoke its name in this house was suspect. And so, Poe's encounters with Sissy, who was really a child, were frozen in an eternal present tense for him. Wedged between what was and what will be. Poe had not yet found a way to accommodate her to his way of looking at the world. His world had to change.

Sissy tucked her body into his. Poe stood coolly. Sissy was purring like a kitten waiting to be petted and combed.

"Would you like to kiss me?" Sissy said.

"Yes," Poe kissed her gingerly because of her tiny frame.

"Why do not we lie down for a moment?" Sissy said.

Poe said all right. He uncovered the bed and she lay down, but she just lay there. Poe started to think: well, she wants to be taken, so he began to kiss her over and over again, and then he started to knead her tiny breasts closest to her heart with his right hand while he was kissing her.

"Make love with me," Poe said.

"I can not, I am marked by the moon," Sissy said. "We can sleep together anyway. I just want to sleep with you and start to know you better. We don't have to hurry too fast about anything." She was the shyest person he had ever been close to. But then she tried to suck the air out of Poe's mouth as if she were losing her own wind, as if she wanted to drink his life in. Poe reeled in counterpoint to her. He composed herself against the reeling of her moist strings. She transformed into the aggressor and began rubbing herself against him, and then pulled away as if in anger. But now Sissy was just unwilling to make love. She wanted to talk under her breath, with her eyes closed, but now Poe could not unwind.

She fell into a nap and Poe lay beside her in the full light of the studio, which seemed as transparent as a fish-bowl. She started murmuring with her eyes shut. Poe reached between her legs but she curled into him like a stray cat. Poe started to whisk her hair, as if he were molding her into someone softer. Poe wanted to brush her back into the past, into her original form, a clean slate. He worked the hair on her nape, brushing her neck, and curled it over. She looked innocent and Poe fantasized rivers of games they could play, not catty or fawning but with intricate complications soaring. Poe suddenly felt old and it was the reason he wanted her young, naive self around. You cannot bury a ghost, Poe told himself, and he left her sleeping.

6 POE MOVES TO PHILADELPHIA

POE, TORMENTED by hunger, left New York in early 1838, to move into a boardinghouse at 202 Mulberry in Philadelphia with his wife Virginia and his mother-in-law Mrs. Clemm.

Poe wrote *William Wilson* and it was published in by William E. Burton in *Burton's Gentleman's Magazine*, telling Poe's story of his conscience as his double, so, when he struggles with his twin selves in Rome, during Carnival, as Wilson is about to seduce a married woman, his double arrives in a mirror and then Wilson utterly murders himself.

When the magazine featured in September 1839 *The Fall of the House of Usher*, his pensive Gothic *chef-d'oeuvre*, this tale was *vis-à-vis* a brother and sister who jeopardized themselves through a miasma in the tarn transforming into supernatural forces marauding them by chance with death-like trances. Poe's *action d'éclat* was honored for the compass of his mind's eye more than the bubble reputation had inclined to him before.

What about the distance that his superior intellect should afford?

To make nothing of his begrudging personality's virulence, his estranged falling-out with society and even his enmity through treating The Narrator as his nearest and dearest enemy.

Through his nascent ruminations he endured the melancholy of his edgy, restless life, soon allotting a morbid tone to the mood of his writing.

You might ask yourself if your respect of your own siblings should occasion your own lift out of trifling mawkishness.

Or if you, too, are linked in a conjugal escapade, could your rational attainments encompass elucidating criminal proof of sophisticatedly hewn paradoxes left behind by astute malefactors?

If a transgressor should cast his shadow across you, could you make out the deceiver and bring him to justice?

So, if you could imagine yourself taking the place of Poe, overcoming the *façade* of evil by feigning allure, by exhibiting a complex identity, with deceit as your weapon, a privation from sorrow or empathy, feeling disposed to *ennui* and reckless toward society. Come ahead, *en revanche*.

Some time drifted by until October 20, 1840 arrived and Burton sold his *Gentleman's Magazine* to George R. Graham. In February 1841, a financial crisis caused Philadelphia banks to stop paying notes higher than five dollars. Poe accepted work from Graham to review books for $800 a year.

In March, Poe's tale *The Murders in the Rue Morgue*, the first to use ratiocination to solve a crime, was typeset. Poe spelled out his story to solve the double murder of Madame L'Espanaye and her daughter.

He realized that he was casting himself as the first expert in raciocination, via the process of exact reflecting through a reasoned train of his inmost thoughts, and his mind was seized as if by an oracle of fuming vapors from the hearing of deaf actions and the seeing of the blind.

Poe rushed in to work at Graham's Magazine. When Poe stepped in, he could hear the clatter of presses being set by hand in cold type. Editors barked. Doors slammed. A copy boy raced upstairs with page proofs, he tripped, and the proofs floated downstairs. Poe left the hand grinding of the presses in the front room as he entered his workplace and climbed upstairs to his desk, through the fluttering clips: Farina cologne water, scythes, mechanical lamp depot, Gillett steel pens are better than quills, Payson's indelible ink, steam ship passage and trains running, baths and miracle cures, theatrical announcements; auction notices; John Anderson Solace Tobacco at John Anderson's Havana Segar Store, NATIONWIDE FINANCIAL CRISIS.

George Graham seized in his hands the clippings and looked askance at Poe's entrance. Graham was Poe's boss and he usually radiated gruff and pompous cynicism as a rule.

"Nationwide Financial Crisis," Graham muttered.

Then Poe saw a burly leatherhead enter, toadying to

Graham. Poe recognized the leatherhead as the 67-year-old droll

chief of the volunteer municipal police force. The leatherhead

nodded, sleepy-eyed and blustering, punch-drunk, but street-smart,

lighting a pristine, fragrant cigar.

"I am the law," the leatherhead arrogantly said, blowing a

fistful of smoke.

Poe, as he absorbed the scent, suggestive to him of opium,

struggled to jolt himself back to real life. He ducked around the

corner of the office and reaching under his desk, he removed from

his carpetbag a continuous scroll of paper, which he had pasted

together at both ends. His eyes were downcast as he took out his

raven-quilled pen and scrawled letters as the first step in

deciphering codes for his column: a = s, b = a, c = u, he wrote.

Then, frustrated, he muttered to himself.

"This is the ugliest hyeroglyphical puzzle I've ever seen,"

Poe said. Then he transformed the letters into a caricature of a

grotesque satanic figure. Poe covered his face with the page as a

mask and grinned sardonically. Then he snapped his fingers as he

realized the connection he had deciphered. He quickly scrawled the correct interpretation and held up the paper triumphantly.

"Unraveled!" Poe said.

Graham still held the financial crisis head clipping as Graham and the leatherhead entered, blustering, peering disdainfully over Poe's shoulder.

"Here, tomahawk man," Graham said to Poe. "Cut the copy to 8 inches."

"Have I been living in a dream?" Poe said as he read the clipping.

"Scribble, scribble, scribble..." the leatherhead said snidely to Griswold.

"You're not from around here, are you?" the leatherhead asked Poe.

"Born in Boston," Poe said.

The leatherhead moved toward Poe menacingly, picking up a clothbound book from Poe's collection as if it were a brick.

"The conchologists book: a system of testaceous malacology, edited by you," the leatherhead read.

Poe picked up a nearby whelk shell and held it to his ear, hearing the raging sound of surf and a distant foreshadowing cry: Eddie. Poe offered the shell it to the leatherhead.

"I solve mysteries," Poe said. "Because mysteries force a man to think. That can injure your health."

Copy editor Rufus Griswold then brought in to Poe fashion illustration proofs. Poe handed Griswold the edited cipher story.

"I do not lay out fashion plates, or edit this sentimental treacle," Poe said to Griswold.

"Not you. You decipher any code and solve any mystery. You weave a web and then you unravel the web," Griswold said, flinching angrily as he exited.

"The mysteries I write make my readers feel like detectives," Poe said. "I am obsessed by tales in which a fragile, delicate woman is drawn into romance, antiquity, chilling suspense and carnal terror."

"The mighty hunter of eyelashes," the leatherhead said.

"I will wager I can solve a real crime," Poe said. But Poe

watched uneasily as Graham and the Leatherhead and Griswold conspired together. "Give me an assignment," Poe said to Graham.

"Internal affairs are none of your business," the leatherhead said under his breath to Graham.

Poe overheard, but maintained a stone face as if he did not.

"I am not in business to make powerful enemies," Graham said to Poe.

Then Graham motioned Griswold into the room with them and closed the door so that the others would not hear. The workers shuffled near the transom so they could hear every word.

"The banks are suspending business," Graham read the page proof to Poe. "Closed. We have to cut your hours."

"I have increased circulation," Poe said.

"You understand," Graham said. "Why don't you come to me with your ideas?"

Poe stormed out.

Griswold slammed the door behind Poe.

"F-f-f-f-fashion plates," the leatherhead taunted Poe.

"I resign," Poe muttered under his breath.

"Literature is his religion," Graham said to Griswold.

"He thinks he is its high-priest with a whip of scorpions," Griswold said to Graham.

Poe's silhouette sat in the street amid the blustering storm of traffic. His carpetbag stood next to him on the ground, spilling 3 shirt collars, a pocket inkstand, a strop and a manuscript that lay unrolled on the ground. The business people walked on. Poe stuffed his belongings back into place.

Poe heard laughter overhead as a hidden piano from another brownstone passionately resonated Franz Liszt

7 SISSY'S SIGNS OF TB

WHEN POE got home, Sissy was rubbing the cat's neck, and behind her ears, and pinching her neck until her eyes would become ecstatic. She would talk her cats more than to him in her sing-song voice and then say, "I think she rather likes it," while she was combing her. Then she started sleeping facing away from him with her back to him snore and the cat huddled up against her. She nurtured her cat in the same way she nursed her grudges against him, tenderly, delicately, not chipping off the tender layers but holding the warmth against her breastbone all night, dreaming her dreams around it, careful not to wake it up, but letting it sleep and twitch and growl. That was a kind of separation.

"I want to tell you a story, Sissy," Eddie said. Sissy was already asleep. "I have been called a visionary and a daydreamer. You should take that with a grain of salt. When I imagine I do it for you, too. I set the stage, its time and circumstances; I introduce the characters and construct them and all that business. But this story I am writing now is true, and it was a crime. I cannot control how they hurt each other because it is over now. They took on passions of their own. I started over at the brooder. And I could see how this precarious and risky shell we live in makes for pleasure and for suffering. What I want is wisdom concerning my origins, experience and knowledge together with good judgment and understanding. I want to know why I was born. And I hope I will find out through this roundabout path. Because sometimes I hear things that no one else in the room hears."

"The loyalty of loved ones in the family and of true friends relieves human suffering in this brutal world.

"I certainly make trouble for myself by ridiculing my competitors, by mocking them, and I always seem to do this at the worst possible time,

"I will say this to the air if I have to, as if words could matter anyway, now or then or ever. Maybe it was bad timing for me to fall in love with you, but when something like this happens, it has always been happening, and it will always be happening.

"This is the way I see God, inside the pain,

"If I can not live here, I will have to live where I can write,

That night Poe remembered that he had always been different from the rest, even as a boy, he was a loner. Poe sneaked out of the boarding house without awakening anyone and played out his fascination with the night by roaming under the moon. He evoked the moon with his pronounced forehead, his aquiline arch, his melancholy eyes and his pale, romantic air.

The foundry seemed odd with its skeletal creations, and the open lot seemed ancient. Reflections glared up from the puddles of water. The water of the North River was beautiful that night, beyond any water that Poe had ever floated in. It was a turquoise that seemed impossible on this planet, a metallic blue-green that was more metallic than liquid. Poe swam in it, floating on his back and watching the stars, tracing the path of the falling stars as they ran from one quadrant to the next, in the great arc above him. He slipped out of the water like a pink chameleon and still naked, built a fire from dead branches. The fire reflected off his skin with an unearthly glow.

Poe sang his songs, and then lowly, chants wailed from the

despair inside him. He would ululate in his otherworldly moan, his lips drawn back in a sardonic grimace, his eyes squinting. Everything that Poe saw was unearthly, the artificially stark moon that exposed but did not warm the surface of the world, with no memory of living things.

His teachers had always persisted with Poe about his attitude, but talking had always been difficult, and advice never had the force of the future because he saw the future with more dread than wisdom.

His best friends had always been gamblers when he was a boy in boarding school. They had usually suffered their punishments alone for playing cards without permission, Poe remembered, and he felt still rubbing the back of his collar against his neck and shrugging his shoulders, thinking, Why am I here?

His teachers had never known where to begin explaining how fast the money could disappear. There was too much to explain to this boy about how the world worked. And the boy both knew too much anyway and still he would never fit in. His teachers had usually begged off with lip service about his poetry and what it meant to them.

Poe walked home to the boardinghouse at 202 Mulberry Street, and soon after, Sissy popped out of bed, hovered wasp like and buzzed around Poe's listless body. She thought Poe had been writing all night. She shook him, but he curled up slyly, pretending to hibernate. Sissy then brushed him away in disgust at his lazy nature and stretched willfully. She jumped with a dancer's leap into the bed and then bounded out of the bed and sailed away from the room.

Sissy entered the kitchen again and pulled open the pantry door. She decided to boil one egg and then changed her mind and puts two eggs on to boil with a conductor's flourish of her wrist. She then peeked around the corner at Poe lying in bed. Sissy came over to Poe and shook him by the shoulders. Poe stirred and reached out sleepily to Sissy, but she then wrestled away and threw a pillow at him. Sissy then raced through the shadowy halls and by the sun-lit windows and doorways in her perpetual cat-and-mouse game of pretending and withholding from him.

The two eggs were roiling around in the boiling water.

Sissy gingerly pulled the two hot eggs out and started breaking her

eggshell away and devouring the egg. The steam started to rise

from the kettle. Poe heard the kettle starting to boil and rolled out

of bed. Sissy heard Poe stirring and realizing that there was only

one boiled egg left and that she was still hungry, she took another

uncooked egg from the counter and whisked it into an egg cup for

Poe just before he entered. Sissy started cracking her egg and

picking up the pieces of her eggshell and she pushed the salt and

pepper to Poe's side of the table. Poe sat down and in his morning

ritual; he pulled the egg and eggcup away from Sissy toward

himself. The steam was rising from the kettle but neither one of

them budged to take it off the flame. Then, when Poe finally

flinched, Sissy rose and prepared the tea. Poe poised to crack his

egg, which lay perched in the eggcup, as Sissy served him his tea.

Sissy sat down across from him and started sipping his tea with a

puckish smile as Poe cracked his egg, and the raw white and runny

yolk spilled out all over his plate. Poe then jumped across the table

to catch Sissy, but she flew away. Poe grabbed after Sissy's skirt

and then jumped up grasping for her leg but she escaped his grip

and Poe was left with the slamming of the door. Poe could hear her running through the hallway overhead and giggling.

Poe watched a silhouette of Sissy transform into a shadow moving on the wall and the wall then transfiguring into a window and her face turned into steam. The steam then began to glow as the sun came up and Poe awakened. He realized that he was sleeping in his study.

Poe realized he sat in his overstuffed chair, wandering in his dreams, with his quill in his hand, no longer scratching.

Poe thought: I am fighting all the time to discover my natural talent and learn how to use it and stay clear of those who waste it and never find out what it is they want. Poe walked downstairs and found Muddie stoking the fire. She sits by me and drinks it all in and then leaves me to my brooding by the brick wall.

At breakfast, Sissy sang a folksong about a mockingbird to Poe as they sat in the boarding house. Sissy was entertaining Poe by moving mechanically as if she were a figure in a music box.

Poe responded ironically and harmonized with Sissy,

improvising a minstrel's soft-shoe.

Sissy's voice faltered and she grasped the sheer window-curtain, coughing into it.

Poe reacted instinctively to catch her.

Sissy reached up for the curtain and while she gasped for air, the curtain was sucked against her face like a blood-soaked shroud.

Poe and Muddie then helped Sissy into the small bed. Sissy sank right there, collapsed and pale under the low ceiling. Poe reached down to Sissie and wiped his bloodied hands. Her hollow, consumptive breathing filled the empty air. Muddie reached out for Poe, urgently and they rose together and walked out to the hall. Her eyes brimmed with tears.

"I'm going out to buy something to help her sleep," Poe said to Muddie as they walked down the stairs together.

"I am not running no hospital here, either," Muddie started to say, pulling Poe closer, softly, blocking his exit, while hiding her daughter's contagion from the neighbors.

"I have used laudanum since I was a baby," Poe said to Muddie.

"No, Eddie," Muddie began sermonizing glumly. "Are you trying to fool me" And then Muddie began to erupt furiously. "Or just fooling yourself?"

Sissy roamed out into the hall, with an abandoned expression on her pale, death-like face.

"I am the head of this household," Poe began to say, but his rage transformed to uncertainty upon seeing Sissy. Sissy moved to Poe and naively tucked herself under his arm.

"What do you think you are doing?" Muddie said to Poe, mocking his old nursemaid's rural accent. "You are not nursing my daughter with laudanum."

"What does it mean, Mama?" Sissy said.

"Opium dissolved in alcohol," Poe said, as he led Sissy to her bed.

"You were always such a quick and clever boy but you were spoiled by your step-parents," Muddie shouted upstairs.

"That is uncalled for," Poe said.

"You were allowed an extravagant amount of pocket money, which enabled you to get into all manner of mischief," Muddie said.

"It was just to make me strong and healthy or to put me to sleep when I was restless backstage," Poe shouted downstairs to Muddie. "What's wrong with peace and quiet?" Then he whispered to Sissy, "And a little mischief."

"That is all it is," Sissy said.

Muddie recognized Sissy's naive frailty. Muddie stomped upstairs then and seized Poe aside.

"Reap the whirlwind," Muddie said to Poe.

Sissy collapsed. Poe and Muddie together carried Sissy to her bed. But she writhed restlessly.

Poe was overcome by concern and he sat down at the foot of the bed and passed his hands across her forehead, intending to mesmerize her. He gazed into her eyes.

"Sleep," Poe said to her.

"I can not," Sissy cried. But her eyes became weary as she approached exhaustion. Her lids quivered. Poe closed them. Her breathing became restful.

"Sissy. Are you asleep?" Poe said. Muddie then bitterly waved Poe away.

"Do not wake me," Sissy said. "Let me die."

8 MARY ROGERS LOSES HER BABY

A FEW weeks later, Anderson and Mary Rogers stood at Wright Winston & Stebbins Dry Goods, 53 Liberty Street, in New York, viewing her new frock. Anderson drew Mary Rogers behind a translucent paper screen, and helped her into her clothes, buttoning the collar of her new willowy brown satin frock. He hung over her arm a black shawl and a blue scarf, and handing her a Tuscan leghorn hat and a light-colored parasol. His large fingers slowly tied a small silk handkerchief around her neck. Then Anderson slipped a paper cigar-band ring over Mary Rogers' finger. She gazed self-consciously at her reflection in the mirror. She bowed and a lock of hair tumbled down, and she loosened a garter, showing her pantolette, and her pale thigh. Anderson took Mary Rogers's fingers then.

"This is for your understanding. I am not some careless, rogue male," Anderson said.

"A gypsy told me I would undergo a transformation this summer," Mary Rogers said. She coquettishly twisted the ring.

"You can not ask ghosts and gypsies for directions concerning your future," Anderson said. "You have to speak to..."

Then the shop clerk interrupted them. Anderson shooed her away.

"Neanderthals!" Anderson muttered. "Middle-class hicks forcing their prejudices..."

Mary Rogers backed away from Anderson's fury. But he advanced and unraveled her hair ribbons.

"I wish I could take your pretty head and see inside it, all your secrets," Anderson said.

"Reading minds is a delicate matter," Mary Rogers said. They laughed together intimately. Then Anderson settled up their account. They could both see Poe through the window.

"What do you make of him?" Anderson asked, as Mary Rogers watched Poe, intrigued. She shook her head, quizzically. "Nathaniel Hawthorne said he is a pure journalist. And clear."

"He looks nervous," Mary Rogers said. Then Anderson and Mary Rogers walked to John Anderson's Havana Cigar Store,

319 Broadway and Thompson. He brought her into his private office in the back room, where he began sweeping his hands through her hair. As Mary Rogers slowly fell back, she watched herself in the mirror. He swung her, tenderly supporting her with one arm. She waved her hand, indicating he should close the drapes and he pulled her closer as she preened.

As Anderson lit a candle, the candle's fluttering broke the shadows. He wound a music box, which played "Children's Games" by Liszt, drowning out the passers-by. The patterns of smoke were transformed into finger-tips tracing rhythms on the bare skin at the back of her neck. Mary Rogers saw her mother's silhouette outside, and heard her rattling the doorknob, but turned away, surrendering to Anderson.

"I do feel like playing," Mary Rogers said.

"What is bothering you?" Anderson said.

"I wish life had a gridiron so I could tell where I was going," Mary Rogers said. She stood near dark, looking out the window of Anderson's shop toward the intersection.

Anderson could see in Mary Rogers's eyes that she was disturbed but worse, he saw the first embers of rage in her eyes.

"Why was I born?" Mary Rogers said. Her eyes were wet but she would not allow tears to form into beads and drop from her eyes and cheeks. She was almost overwhelmed from fighting it.

"The last time I saw my mother and father together with us children, she was pitching her bare feet down the stairs from the boardwalk first and then running downhill across the gritty beach and diving into the roiling surf where I saw her swallowed by waves and I gasped and I jumped up and cried out "Ma-Ma!" I was relieved to see her spring up again in the surf. Then I watched her vanish again. And I lost my breath. But then she would bob back up and then disappear and return, over and over. Anderson began to rub Mary Rogers's shoulders.

"You are always hatching a plot to complicate my life," Anderson said, "A plot like solitaire betrayed. He touched her gently because his hands felt thick against her petite frame. "What are you thinking about so hard?" It was no good. She could not relax.

Mary Rogers felt she was locked in a dream. Dreams cannot be shared, torn apart and sorted out and analyzed to find out what they might mean. She felt that if she revealed her dreams to Anderson he would force her to change and compromise. She smiled shyly.

"Have I held you back?" Anderson said.

"Do not stab out at me," Mary Rogers said. "There has got to be give and take."

"That is just what I expected," Anderson said. He was infuriated.

"You did not hear me," Mary Rogers said. "You always run out. Look at you. You are ready to go again. You hide. What are you hiding from?"

"At least I am not like Poe," Anderson said.

"What is wrong with him?" Mary Rogers said.

"He is too much in his head," Anderson said. "When someone is like that, people think he is hiding something."

"It is all right," Mary Rogers said. "People get trapped by

words sometimes, like procrastination. That was in my horoscope. Ruminating about the past. And when you live in the past you are in an imaginary place. I get off the track like that sometimes and try to make things over in my mind..."

"Just wait," Anderson said. "You have a lot of living ahead of you. You will see. It just takes time. You have to be driven to get anywhere in this world."

Mary Rogers's ears were ringing. She avoided his glance. He appeared both deferential and scornful.

"What is the matter?" Mary Rogers said. She felt like giving up on the whole arrangement. After all the work I have done for him, we are not communicating. We cannot connect. I feel like I should say something but I cannot think of anything to say and then I feel strange and alienated.

"Why should I care about you anyway?" Anderson said. "I can not meet you anymore. We are not getting anywhere trying to work out our problems in public for everyone to see. If you want to meet me in your in your dreams I can not stop you, but don't make me a target for scorn in public. You are too dependent on other people for things you could do yourself."

"We have not really been together since that night a long time ago when I thought I was pregnant," Mary Rogers said. "There has been a gap between us."

"Everything has changed," Anderson said. "And I do not like newshounds like Poe overshadowing us. He has come between us."

"What are you so angry about?" Mary Rogers wanted to know.

"You never listen," Anderson said.

"Listening isn't like that," Mary Rogers said. "You hear something and then turn it against me."

"I am not the guilty one," Mary Rogers said. "I have not done anything wrong. Stop trying to change me." She had a bitter tone in her voice. "I am not your puppet."

"You work for me," Anderson said. "You make your feelings match the part I want you to play. I want you to become somebody, something more."

"I know a turning point when I see it," Mary Rogers said. "I have lost my faith in the power of friendship. You learned something and so you changed. I hope you are the better man for it."

"I will not be changed by circumstances outside of my control," Anderson said.

"I do not want to see my real life played out on this stage," Mary Rogers said. "In this middle class location of all places? Do you have some underlying logic behind all the illogical and absurd things you make me do? Have I done something to deserve this? I am expected to believe you will keep my feet on the ground. I have to take all of this on faith. I am expected to believe in you on faith without any proof. Thank you, Mr. Anderson for your infinite wisdom?"

Mary Rogers closed her eyes and struggled to forget the strangest dream of all, a recurring nightmare. Some customers then called Anderson away to the front of the store.

Mary Rogers opened up the door to the loading dock and walked out into the fresh air to let the cool night air in her lungs. She tried to draw a bead on the stars that made up the crab with her thumb and forefinger she could not connect the glimmering dots. After awhile her eyes were strained and she blotted them out with her fingers. She was reeling from feelings of sorrow for the loss of her self.

When Anderson came out to the dock, Mary Rogers said, "Would you like to hear my secret?" Then she whispered in his ear. "I am not sure if there is life after death. I want to have children so that part of me lives on." Anderson moved away from her nervously. She held out her arms, longing for an embrace.

"I think my trouble comes from working in this false facade, with you geared up in some middle-aged banker's outfit," Mary Rogers blurted out. "I do not need more barriers to openness and vulnerability." She fought her jumbled emotions that conflicted with each other, emotions like the love and the hate she felt for him. "Do you want to know what Poe told me?" Anderson nodded.

"The halcyon is the bird who calms the wind," Mary Roger said. "But when she was about to breed, even she needed a nest. She feared the hunters stalking on dry land, so she found a snug harbor on a rock over-hanging the water and burrowed in. One day she flew out fishing for dinner to feed her brood, and while she was searching over the sea, gliding a mile a minute as she does, a wave crashed over the nest. So when she returned with the fish in her beak, and her heart fluttering with love for her little ones, she found them washed far away and the sea which was to be her refuge had drowned her babies and proved more treacherous than hunters stalking her on dry land."

"I am not taking advantage of you," Anderson said. "Just concentrate on that for now." He felt her tenseness in his own fiber.

"You have got a lot of potential, but you are not applying yourself," Anderson muttered.

Mary Rogers wished it would rain.

"We will both be lonely forever," Mary Rogers said.

"You are too seductive to ever be lonely," Anderson said.

Mary Rogers wheeled away from Anderson. He grabbed her forearm and then stopped her other arm from lashing out.

"I thought you would make me a success, too," Mary Rogers said.

"I want us to work together," Anderson reminded her.

"Is my craving affection so obvious?" Mary Rogers asked Anderson.

"My conscience dictated I should mask my true desires for you, and so I have been silent," Mary Rogers said. "But I want to show you who I am and how I feel about you. I do not want this to be over." Mary Rogers closed her eyes and the image from the nightmare passed through her mind, the canopy above their shared bed fluttered like a ghostly scrim. A coal train wailed. Mary Rogers teetered on the edge of the oblong box.

Mary Rogers felt herself lured out of her shell. The last of the daylight leaked in from the west and the air appeared dark and smoky and dusty.

"Do you want me to keep it a secret that we are going to have a baby?" Mary Rogers said.

"Be my guest," Anderson said. Mary Rogers felt the

distance between them like a race with the devil. She knew he would require more careful diplomacy now. She felt awkward.

"You had an affair with a married woman one time," Mary Rogers said.

"Are you thinking of having an affair?" Anderson said.

"Why are you acting like you can read my mind?" Mary Rogers said. "I told you I could not promise perfection." Anderson was surprised when he looked at Mary Rogers and she had tears in her eyes. "I am not dishonest."

"I feel like a fool," Anderson said. He was fierce and frustrated. "You just counted off the ways to waste my money."

Mary Rogers wondered, why do I resurrect old characters like Anderson and try to patch them together? Am I trying to pass him off as new? To erase my own face? Am I the self-effacing ghost? She was choked by repressed histrionics. Am I just playing at love he can win?

"Get off my back," Mary Rogers said.

"You sound suicidal," Anderson said. "Here, let me get

you a gun."

"You should go away for a week or two," Mary Rogers whispered to Anderson.

"Give me back my real life," Mary Rogers said.

"You are too late," Anderson said. "Are you trying to fool me or fooling yourself? You have not lived up to my expectations. We are incompatible."

"I am changing," Anderson said.

"People never change," Mary Rogers said. "You are living proof. You didn't feel like connecting to me when you met me and you do not now. That has not changed."

"Do you want to go through with this?" Anderson said.

"I wish I had something nice to wear," Mary Rogers said.

"Did I just buy you something?" Anderson said.

"You know I love you, but things have to change." She walked back into the shop and made busy-work for herself around the place. She begins rummaging through a trunk of clothes he had bought for her to wear at work. "What do you think?" Mary

Rogers asked Anderson when he came in.

"I like it. Keep it," Anderson said.

Mary Rogers started to throw it out.

"What are you doing?" Anderson said. They played tug-of-war with the dress. Then Mary Rogers threw out the sweater. Anderson tried to make peace by hugging her but she resisted him. "Throw it out," he relented. This masquerade was her game, Anderson knew, inconsistent emotionally, alternatively withholding her love and then generous, struggling to keep her secret and then loosing her sexuality. Tonight Anderson was intrigued. Mary Rogers scorned him at times like this. She knew Poe's dream world was another imaginary world, but it was Anderson's practicality that made her anxious and angry now. She created distance and with that distance she was saying that she expected and needed him to be strong, materialistic, business-like and practical so that she could be feminine and impulsive. Then after Mary Rogers had considered this emotional whirlpool, she looked up, pleased with herself.

Anderson reacted with anxiety, restlessness, stressed voice, wide eyes, and moist hands.

"If you have a boy, he had better look like both of us," Anderson said. "You are not sure? Charming. O.K. What am I getting into?"

"I am in search of my soul," Mary Rogers said. "If some part of me lives on after death, is that part that lives on my children?"

"Look," Anderson said, "You provoke, subtly, anxiety and dissension in me by your unwillingness to give."

Mary Rogers twisted her hands into fists and then rubbed them into her eyes in an attempt to control her anger. "Why did you cast me in this role? You're going to split us up and foul up any relationship I may have with you and you are splitting me into little pieces inside, too!"

"I love warring internal emotions," Anderson said, sarcastically.

"I do not want to get hurt again," Mary Rogers said.

"You are strong enough to resolve this conflict," Anderson

told Mary Rogers. "But you don't know it yet." Then he exited and asked her to lock up when she went out. She saw his shadowy form walking away. She raced out and caught up with him near the street corner, and dragged him back in the door of the shop.

"I am almost twelve weeks pregnant," Mary Rogers said to Anderson. He offered encouragement with his hand on her shoulder. "What do you think about the name..." she started to say, but she could see that Anderson was preoccupied.

"Excuse me," Mary Rogers said. She walked to the next room. When she returned she looks pale and wan.

"What is the matter?" Anderson asked her. He put his arm around her shoulders but she shrugged it off.

"I am bleeding," Mary Rogers said. "I have to call a doctor."

"I know someone," Anderson said. "Just to be on the safe side."

Then Anderson closed up his shop and walked Mary Rogers to the Hoboken ferry terminal. Mary Rogers was sicker when they arrived in Hoboken. Anderson found a Carman who took them up to Nick Moore's Tavern. When they arrived at the raucous roadhouse, Mrs. Kellenbarach greeted whispered to Anderson at the door. Then she led Mary Rogers upstairs. Mary Rogers's face was somber. Kellenbarach brought her into her own grand German-made bed.

"Let me see you," Mrs. Kellenbarach said.

Mary Rogers was twisted with agony.

"You are blutbefleckt," Mrs. Kellenbarach said. "This is your bed. My mother was so before with me."

"I am scared," Mary Rogers said. "I am very cold."

Kellenbarach covered Mary Rogers with a quilt and propped her up in front of the window to watch the North River. Mary Rogers felt a relentless backward pull from deep inside her groin. The night was white with overcast. Mary Rogers could see on the hill the monastery. A castle, she thought, made of gray granite. She through the highest window a candle moving, casting shadows which streaked the walls with liquid smoke. Someone walked through the long halls, passing lonely corridors. Mary Rogers heard her own overworked breathing and felt in her heart the cold dark that is defeat. She saw hanging on the wall a crucifix made of smooth blond wood. This night will be my pilgrimage, and in the morning it will be over, she pretended. She heard the shrill and raucous party downstairs and she felt the distance made bitter by this deathly place by the lonely shadows and by her own hard breathing. Even her little prayers were unfamiliar and hard. The rough woman Kellenbarach came through the door again and Mary Rogers sat silent and pale. It seemed the real world had been made a desperate, vain place. It seemed everyone else had all the time in the world and Mary Rogers had only shadows in her imagination of the baby inside her and only the form of her bones beneath the covers. The whole place seemed built on Kellenbarach, someone else's, dull primitive magic that just was not an answer now. This rough woman has faith, so I will have faith in her. So Mary Rogers sat, silent and pale.

"I do not belong in this reckless place," Mary Rogers said in her ecstasy of fear. She hoped Kallenbarach would take that for strength.

"I am helping you," Kallenbarach said. "This is vergänglich, this trouble."

"You have all the time in the world," Mary Rogers said.

Kallenbarach flung back the covers. The sheets were soaked through with watery blood. The sky overhead roiled gray. Mary Rogers looked up hopefully. Kallenbarach's expression was eerie.

"Be brave," Kallenbarach said. "Have faith."

I am not nervous, Mary Rogers thought, because she was. This is not good. Mary Rogers's face suddenly twisted in pain from fighting tears and panic. She remembered a nightmare image that made her dizzy, an image from when she was a little girl of Red Riding Hood, but she felt so childish, she blocked it out. She felt she had jumped into a roiling cyclone, and she was searching in the image for the unborn baby.

There is a place for unborn babies to rest, Mary Rogers thought, the moon finds them a place. Her face was stricken gray by discontent. She no longer wished to live. I am going hunting for his spirit. Am I crazy now? How will I know him if I do find him?

Mary Rogers saw in her feverish pain her double. Is that you? She thought. But it was Anderson.

9 MARY ROGERS MEETS THE GYPSY

MARY ROGERS was sitting in front of the gypsy. The gypsy was reading her tarot cards.

"I know what I have to do," Mary Rogers said when she saw the card.

"The death card," the gypsy said. "It will be a slow death." The gypsy tried to calm Mary Rogers then by placing her fingers on her hand. "But that may only mean it will be a slow change. The change has to completely come from you. Your struggle is with the flip side of the card. You have trouble letting them both happen at the same time. Fire sign and water sign. But the two sides can co-exist. When you decide to make the change, it means just letting what is there surface. New habits, new attitudes, let them mingle with what you already believe instead of falling and rebuilding. Can you handle the pain of changing?"

"I do not want to be captured and closed in," Mary Rogers said. "Will having this baby be too much for this shaky bond with him? I started on this path at birth, allowing outside forces to be more powerful than my inside forces."

"You have to allow the light to come through," Mary Rogers said. "Good outweighs evil. You are a positive influence on people. The blame you put on yourself is wrong. It is never right. You should always depend on yourself."

"Can I depend on him?" Mary Rogers asked the gypsy. "Will he keep me under his thumb or push me down?"

"Free yourself," the gypsy said. "Your thinking is too rigid."

"I can not think your way," Mary Rogers said.

"I meant to take on a little simple work," Mary Rogers said. "When I met him, I mean. See? This is how the baby is resting in my belly. What does he have to offer this child, anyway? What is his inheritance? What is your vision of my son's future? A nice, quiet paradise? A pigeonhole? Let me feel you." Mary Rogers's eyes focused far away into the ideal beyond. Baby, I am lost in this briar patch, how can I bring you here to this hardscrabble earth.

Mary Rogers was adrift on a sea of forgetfulness, waiting for Anderson to come and rescue her, though her unborn son's ghost haunted her in her dreams.

I want you to live, little baby, I do not want you to miss anything. But I do not want to lose my partner on this seesaw. I know that I want some part of me to never say die, to cheat death, to last, to make a difference in this world. I may be down and flat broke now, but I will make a comeback and I want you to come along with me. You will see.

"I am scared of being weird at birth but at the same time I can not wait to open the package," Mary Rogers said.

"Was and will be are moving toward us all the time," the gypsy said.

"We are too much alike, Anderson, and me" Mary Rogers said. "Always trying to get ahead."

"If you take a chance on a man he makes everything risky," the gypsy said.

"I just want to bring someone new into this crazy world,"

Mary Rogers said. "You bring someone new into this world just so he can take everything you have got and bury you some day."

"Men search for a woman like you," the gypsy said.

"He is a demon one minute..." Mary Rogers said.

"I sense someone enigmatic, someone cryptic," the gypsy said.

"There is a man..." Mary Rogers said.

"He is cocksure," the gypsy said.

"He said to me once he would give me a clue to what he was thinking," Mary Rogers said. "Overconfident, rapacious, glossy ink-black rattling corvine, eager for gratification."

The gypsy held up her hands in dismay and then realized the solution, "Raven. Do not play games with this one. He is a dreamer," the gypsy said. "One man is a puzzler. The other brews passions you can not control within yourself."

"My father once told me 'we inherit the sins of our fathers,' " Mary Rogers said. "Before he sailed away." Mary Rogers had been concentrating so severely that she had wrung her neck into a migraine. She began suffering a visual illusion that only she could see out of the corner of her eye. It was a rippling fiery form shaped like a diamond-backed rattlesnake. The snake called up from inside of her a terror of nothingness, sickness, evil and death, of chaos and formlessness and the burning darkness. She put her hands over her ears and she heard a rush. "Maybe this is my calling," Mary Rogers said sarcastically. "Maybe I have to live with that man of passion, take him to bed with me every night."

"Do not block out your heart of hearts," the gypsy said.

"I just want my true despair... "Mary Rogers said. "I mean my true desire... "She laughed. "I do not know my own mind anymore. Of course if the man of passion wants to, he can burrow inside me and change me around to his liking. He can make me into a killing machine, if he wants to. He can manipulate me any way he wants. Who I am if I can be changed against my will at his impulse? Everybody is always trying to change my mind, or to affect my opinion. I do not even know my own mind anymore."

"By accident or providence, you have come across these two men," the gypsy said. "Just turn loose of those old resentments and you will be free."

I ran across this book."

Mary Rogers's face brightened then and she became more resolute.

"My prospects are not so grim," Mary Rogers said.

"Passion will not kill you," the gypsy said. "You can rise above these circumstances."

"I am still a wandering soul," Mary Rogers said.

"Go, with my blessing," the gypsy said.

"I have my problems, but I am not crazy," Mary Rogers said. "I can not get to the point where I am beat down. I feel like I am under sea-water sometimes."

"I just wish I had another chance with my man of passion," Mary Rogers said.

"I have high hopes for you," the gypsy said. "A lot of people never even have one love, and you have more. Find your purpose and abide by that."

The moon floated whiter than new snow on a raven's back, above the wild reality of Manhattan's gas lights, spires, battlements and the white sails rocking in the bay.

"I want to leave this boarding house," Mary Rogers said. "I am tired of fighting with you, mama. Can you not understand that? I am sorry. I want to elope."

"With who? Not him," Phoebe Rogers said. "You should go back to bed and get a good night's sleep. You have to work in the morning."

"My bag is packed and ready," Mary Rogers said.

"You need to wake up about the relationship you have with Mr. Anderson," Phoebe Rogers said. "He is married. He has gripped you in a horrible nightmare. This see-saw you are riding with him is out of balance."

In the morning, Phoebe Rogers put out a new placard at the entrance to her boarding house at 114 Pitt Street, which read: boarding, large rooms, bedroom and pantry attached. She heard the grandfather clock ticking resonantly, saw the light reflected from its crystalline faceted window in its coffin-like cabinet, and felt an intense loneliness. She looked up anxiously at the grandfather clock's eerie face.

"Mary?" she said. But all she heard was the grandfather clock ticking louder. She saw standing behind the translucent glass a shadowy form. She heard a flutter and wheeled around but saw only a rushing flock of birds crossing the window. She looked into the mirror, seeing Mary Rogers beside her, but when she turned, Mary had vanished. She opened the door, but only heard the racket in the street. She was soaked in nervous sweat. She returned and looked into Mary Rogers's empty room. The clock ticked and ticked and ticked.

Phoebe Rogers rushed out to the Broadway and Ann Street Coach Terminal, amid a tide-swell of pedestrians crossing, which abruptly stopped her.

A man offered an open briefcase full of paste jewelry to her.

"Do you want to buy a diamond necklace?" the man asked. His voice was high and hoarse and heavily accented.

"No," Phoebe Rogers brushed him away.

"Do you want to buy a baby?" he said.

Phoebe Rogers was alarmed and hurried on.

In John Anderson's Havana Segar Store at 319 Broadway and Thompson, Phoebe Rogers discovered the store was closed for business. Anderson could see Phoebe Rogers through the shutters, rushing over to the front door of his store. He was surprised, though, when she rushed in through the loading dock.

"I am searching for Mary," Phoebe Rogers said.

"I sent her home after work," Anderson lied.

"I am afraid," Phoebe Rogers explained.

Phoebe caught herself crying, and losing her self-control.

"You do not think she vanished," Anderson said. "She may be home. You should go out now. Excuse me."

Anderson locked the door behind Phoebe Rogers. She stood outside at the entrance to Anderson's shop, puzzled.

The morning of July 29, 1841, John Anderson returned to

his house and undressed himself. He hung his clothes on a chair at the foot of the bed. He bathed his shoulders and neck and rubbed spirits on his neck because his neck felt stiff. He left his trousers on his dressing table, which stood by the foot of his bed. Anderson fell into a fitful sleep, but arose at the first breakfast bell at seven o'clock.

10 POE SEARCHES FOR MARY ROGERS

AT THE Arcade Bath, Number 39 Chambers Street, Poe stood talking to James Gordon Bennett opposite the rotunda, observing that the bank across the street was closed for business.

"Market Crashes!" a newsboy hawked the story.

Poe gazed down at the business plan he was carrying.

"I am looking for work again," Poe explained. "Will you put in a good word for me to Snowden?"

"Yes, of course," Bennett said, as they began walking inside the front, through a gothic arcade built on pillars.

Poe shook hands with Bennett then, and slipped inside the shady vestibule to inhale the vapors. He stood by Greek statues of male figures and a female nude of Diana and then stepped into the steamy air, and he took off his boots, and he felt the clammy mosaic-tiled floor. Poe saw through the steam Griswold and James Gordon Bennett and Snowden shaking hands and standing together.

"Mr. Bennett, publisher of 'City Intelligence', and The New York Herald, and a notorious hoaxer," Snowdon said cynically.

Poe saw the publishers and editors stop at the edge of the marble roman-style impluvium, from which rose warm, sulphurous vapor, which they inhaled. Then he saw John Anderson approaching through the steam.

"Gentlemen, John Anderson, tobacconist," Bennett said gruffly to Griswold.

"I heard you are expecting to entertain Charles Dickens during his tour, Anderson," Snowden said. He expected Anderson to respond proudly, but Anderson appeared shaken.

"What is wrong?" Bennett asked Anderson.

"I have got a problem at my shop," Anderson said. "That cigar girl who ran the shop for me has vanished."

"Now you really need a friend in the press. Have you placed a notice in the papers?" Snowden asked.

"I will pay a hundred for an advertisement seeking

information concerning her whereabouts. I am preparing my run for mayor. I can not afford a whiff of scandal," Anderson said.

Poe heard. Tibbs, lurking in the shadows, overheard also.

At the corner newsstand, later, Poe ran into Tibbs as Tibbs was carrying proofs of The New York Herald: EXTRA! New York Herald CIGAR GIRL VANISHES.

"John Anderson is looking for someone to solve this mystery. Now," Tibbs said to Poe.

"I could solve this mystery. That would sell copy, too," Poe said.

"Did I see you with Bennett?" Tibbs said. Poe remained composed and aloof. "That Bennett is a reptile, you know."

"Magazines. They could all go up in smoke," Poe said. Then Poe saw Snowden appear from around the corner and buy a paper.

"I heard the United States Bank has suspended paying notes of a higher denomination than five dollars. Money is difficult to obtain, even at a high premium," Snowden said.

Snowden caught Poe's eye and Tibbs's eye and pointed to the closed bank, and headline.

"So how shall we turn back the tide?" Poe said.

"Come work for me at the Ladies Home Companion," Snowden said.

"I would like to work with you. Thank you. I have got a story idea that I can nail. Anderson's cigar girl has vanished," Poe said. "I heard a rumor that John Anderson was held for questioning, but discharged for lack of evidence."

"Edit for me and I will print your story. Meet me at the office in the morning," Snowden said.

"I will find out where John Anderson's cigar girl has gone, and why," Poe said.

"Nine o'clock and all is well," Poe heard the leatherhead sing out from his watch house sentry box.

That is a good omen, Poe thought, laughing to himself, because he was wary of any forewarning due to its ironic twin, foreshadowing. He was alert and skeptical of any kind of tip on the stock market or insider's gibberish, because it changed with the wind.

Poe walked into Five Points, the five streets creating a lopsided star out of Cross, Anthony, Little Water, Orange and Mulberry Streets, in a rookerie crawling with gangs: The Roach Guards, the Shirt Tails, the Irish Sluggers, the Dead Rabbits, and the Plug Uglies. The gangs might lurk in any shadow, armed with bludgeons, brickbats and boots studded with hobnails for stamping.

Near a green grocer's which peddled cheap liquor in the back, Poe saw a man squatting between two wagon, with what appeared to be a swatch of blanket over his head, to hide his shame. He squatted like an apoplectic mosquito, hunched over at his filthy business. It was just a glance in the dark, but it played out Poe's horror. He looked again, with a sense of disgust and his perception burrowed further down into his consciousness, into a deeper dread.

There was a man bent down over another man in the dark shadows. The man underneath was squirming as if he was being tickled in a children's game, but it was not like that. The man

underneath was trying to brush away the real flesh and bone. Poe
could see the man on the top was brushing his arm as if he were
cleaning a slate and making it all O.K. His gestures were so light
and poetic that they seemed like mime, but they were what he was
doing to wipe away death's fidgety hands from his skinny frame.

Was that a knife in that man's hand? Poe could barely
make it out, was it going in and in again and again over and over
something like: one, one, one, one, one. Poe reached in and
grabbed the forearm of the man on top. Poe was thinking, once
you know who is your killer, why can you not fight him off? The
killer raced away in a flurry of grunts and the victim was angry
with Poe for driving him away.

"I was getting the better of him," the street fighter said.
Poe backed away, his memory sprouting again from his own
childhood like an awful black mushroom in his brain that was still
growing, and when his memory connected to the present,
everything that was outside was inside, like the evils that shadows
perform here. It was only possible to avoid things; it was never
possible to stop things once they had started. When I start an

argument with Sissy, Poe thought, my beauty, my smooth iris with her smooth and sleek and fragrant petals, I always think I should just go. And then the next time that I wake up, she is gone like a fresh wind when the window's been slammed down. When it starts happening, it is in my tissue and substance and the grain of the world inside the foundation of the world.

When I get the fear like this, Poe thought, it is me that is the root of the fear, and I keep flirting with the fear, and it is the fear of being alive and living and trying to do something new or anything for the first time, or erasing or correcting anything.

On Mulberry Street flies were dancing back and forth in front of Poe's face as he brushed his hand with a whisking rhythm. There were tiny little laudanum bottles tossed along the sidewalk, like remnants of some dead zone culture.

A prostitute in a sparkling blue outfit more underwear than dress, skirted Poe's way.

"Where you going? The prostitute whispered to Poe. Her wig was swooped out. She continued talking under her breath. Poe walked on.

He saw a handbill tacked to the wall saying there was a meeting so the people could discuss the killing. Poe felt more like an outsider now. Who am I to pass out morals in print? Poe thought. He looked in on the block meeting anyway, and saw a disorganized grass-roots affair. He saw people he knew, Mimi, and Rosie in her dust-red housecoat, and three heavily-accented old ladies. They were scared of prostitution, plus the backlash they might get from speaking out against it. A woman took attendance. There were about fifty people. Then Rosie hinted under her breath that maybe the meeting had been infiltrated, as if there might be goons.

"Be careful what you say, we do not know everybody here," Mimi peered around the faces.

"He is not here," Rosie said, slipping the worry off her shoulders, and sighed. Who works for them? Poe wondered, the police? The mayor? The morals squad? Newspaper writers? Me? But he left early, walking out into the blackness and a string on gas-lights, few and far between like pearls glowing in the dark. Maybe this life is just preparation for the next stop down the line.

That night Poe walked through the shadows of cold brick and wood buildings, hearing mechanical strains of music and seeing downtown's dull glow, like sulphur. The world spun beneath him on different tracks, rusting iron or muddy paths and he walked alone. Poe thought he heard a woman's voice pleading for help. He continued walking past a sliding door, unsure if he had heard the voice at first.

"Help me. Can somebody not help me? I am locked in here. Somebody please." Poe started searching for a way to let her out. Then in the next few steps, he came up against a guard in a tired uniform, sagging like a wet camel.

"Somebody is trapped behind that door. She is calling out for help," Poe told the old guard.

"What?" the sleepy guard asked Poe. Poe told him again and again. Finally he understood. "Who is that?" the sleepy guard called to the door. Then Poe could hear something he recognized in the muffled tone of the voice.

"Someone will let you out in just a minute," Poe shouted to the door.

"It is dark," the woman's voice said. "I am locked in here and there is no way out." When the guard unlocked the door, Poe recognized Elizabeth. She was an actress. Elizabeth grabbed Poe's hand and pulled him over to Theater Row. They ducked in the back door of Elizabeth's show.

"What were you doing in there?" Poe said.

"Tomorrow's another day," Elizabeth said to herself, cryptically. She and Poe were standing backstage. The orchestra was playing a harmonic melody that rang like chimes in a window. Poe recognized the set for "The Duchess of Malfi."

"What story are you working on now?" Elizabeth said.

"Have you heard about this cigar girl who vanished?" Poe said. "She was working at John Anderson's cigar store."

"No sooner met but they looked, no sooner looked but they loved ... They are in the very wrath of love," Elizabeth said. "If you come with me sometime, I will show you a place," Elizabeth said.

"What is it called?" Poe asked.

"This is a place where people lose their pain," she said.

"I. Don't. Think. So," Poe said it clearly, with sharp inflections. The street was dark, darkness he knew too well.

"You are not suspicious? Is that it? Why don't you trust people? You should try to trust people, Eddie," she said.

"Tomorrow I will start trusting people," Eddie said.

She was swabbing her face with cotton and fixing her make-up.

"I do not know why you always act like a victim," she muttered. "For Christ's sake! You do not have to take everything so personally." She embraced Poe and then she twirled back onstage. "Do you still act?"

Poe looked at her with a cold, flat expression. "You are joking," Poe said.

When Elizabeth had gone onstage, Poe recognized with familiarity the make-up and had an idea. He sat down at her mirror and began transforming his face into a wild caricature of himself. When he was through, and he would be transformed into his dark twin, disguised as Mr. Thaddeus K. Peasley.

Poe knew how to paint his face because his parents were actors. Even after they had died while he was still an infant, he would often stop by Theater Alley at night to listen in on the latest productions. Everyone in the business knew him and the stage managers would let him look in from backstage.

Poe saw ominous ropes and pulleys weighing down in the darkness from fly lines overhead. Shadows gave way to dim light revealing the intricate shadows of backstage. The stage manager pulled up on the ropes and an arch-shaped drop cloth made its vertical ascent and then gave way to a backdrop that then gave way to a cyclorama. Each successive motion reminded Poe that many things in this labyrinthine place were illusory.

Then Poe entered the paint room workshop further backstage and the gaslights severed the darkness in dribs and drabs. Poe was surprised at the magical drama of the operatic theatrical set pieces arising from the background of the paint room. On the floor stood what appeared to be the murky opening of a secretive tunnel but turned out to be a built unit backed by struts.

His gaze climbed up past the built unit, which was appeared to be a prehistoric stone outcropping.

The edifice was gutted and deteriorating and the cosmetics of the once pristine ivory palisades were chipping off and had been gutted. Poe lifted one of the pillars and moved it away. Behind it was a sketch of Embarkation for Cythera, by Watteau. Poe pushed a paint trolley out of his way. Poe felt like a man walking through someone else's dream.

Poe imagined Mary Rogers, lying hunched up restlessly in a fetal position, tossing and turning. The yellow and purple and red flowers were wrinkled into shadows by her twisting torso and fretting legs. Her long thin fingers kneaded the flowers into wrinkles in her distorted dance. Mary Rogers wrung her hands as you might twist a washrag dry. Mary Rogers had not yet found the part that was meant for her, she had not yet found the mask that was meant for her. The woman inside her was struggling for life.

Her face, which was striking, was searching the dark inside her with disbelief. Her head was buoyed up on her arm; the waves of her shadowy hair were falling across it. She struggled to rest, to solve her internal problems.

Poe heard the actors on stage but he could not stand to think of himself jumping around like a puppet on the stage reciting lines that were put into his mouth. They would have just come out stilted and hobbling. Poe could hear the actor onstage, his voice heavy with earnest over-eagerness and histrionics, choking on strident syllables. Poe winced. He recalled standing exposed onstage and wrestling with his face as it flushed and grimaced against the words he was straining to pronounce. Poe recognized the first act of this cheerless production in this drafty theater. Poe imagined Mary Rogers entering stage right and accepting the new temporary life offered her. Mary Rogers began to confess to Poe's dark spirit.

"I jumped into Anderson's life," Mary Rogers said. "His friends. His business. I was living out the most romantic fantasy that had ever happened to me. We would have lunch together. His face had character and his hands were soft and gentle. He was like a guardian angel." Mary Rogers seemed to swoon in a woozy haze.

"But then he turned away from me," Mary Rogers explained. "He was jealous of every man I spoke to. We stopped speaking. Or we I fended off his craving questions. To be shadowed by this brooding silent devil. I did not know what to do. There are no guardian angels. I knew I had to take care of myself. I could not live under any man's wing.

"The afternoon it ended, it was starting to sprinkle outside, and I thought: 'He's going to try and get me alone.' I had never seen him so nervous. Then, all of a sudden, Anderson and I were alone. We came to a dark thicket and he forced me up against the tree, and brushed up against me. He started humming nonsense about clairvoyance. And I thought: 'you had this all planned out. In the dark.' But of course I was just being hopeful.

"When he started petting me, I just gave in. I do not know what made him break it off between us. His hands were on my throat then, twisting against the grain.

"The last time I saw him was just before sundown when the sky in the west looked, like that back-drop if it were scrawled red and blue with chalk. There were millions of starlings ranging like a cloud, swooping toward me in a wave of little wings. The last thing I heard was a child playing hide-and-seek: you are it!

"I my eyes and I watched him gong away from me and straightening his clothes. I thought this is the real you. It was so unfulfilling and final. That is the way it was meant to be. There are no guardian angels. I have to do it for myself now."

Poe could hear backstage the music in the hall taking its cues in synch with the action of a trap opening beneath the stage, and the rams shoving up a lift by the action of a crank that hoisted up a column.

Poe took one last glance back at Elizabeth onstage. He knew how she must feel, appearing in an out of the way, hole-in-the-wall theater. Poe felt the actors and the actresses all looked very, very tall, because the ceiling of the studio theater was so short. The ceiling was coated with dust like the clay in a mud-dauber's nest. The groggy heat was clabbered close. Elizabeth fanned herself with a frantic stroke and the people in the audience were fanning themselves also. Poe took the chance to gulp down a breath. A big lug entered stage right brandishing a sword. He spoke his lines in an adenoidal drone. Poe hated him. I

could use a glass of air, Poe thought. Elizabeth primped and

flourished like a flower. She looked offstage at Poe, saw that he

had transformed himself into character and winked. Then she

walked over to the wings and whispered to Poe.

"You have changed," Elizabeth said. "I love it the way you

start oozing masculinity when you are mad." Poe walked out as

Peasely, oozing.

Poe strode out forcefully in character, through the 89

degrees of muggy, brooding atmosphere. He walked across to

Corporation Wharf on Vesey Street, and he ducked into the alley

nearby. He looked up, at the luminous dots of gas lamps against

the eerie, overcast sky. He gazed west, through the sfumato,

hearing in the distance cotton bales off-loaded, and cawing gulls,

plunging down through the mist. His boots kicked away the

pigeons that cluttered the theater alley. Poe walked up nodded to

the lamplighter doing maintenance work on his gas lamp.

"Thaddeus K. Peasley," Poe said, introducing himself.

"Have you heard of John Anderson?"

"The tobacco merchant?" the lamplighter asked. He reached up into the glaring vapor and snuffed out the gas lamps' flames. "He owns more of this island than God does."

Poe walked to the Cortland Street Ferry House, where he heard 4 bells from the bridge of the Hoboken ferry. On the wharf, he heard the ring and pawl and ratchet and yanking up of mooring lines to grip the ferry safely bumping in its slip after a safe crossing. The passengers stepped off of the rocking ferry one by one. Poe reacted curiously, seeing what was in one sailor's hand and then he asked to see the sailor's cigar wrapped with the label: Anderson's Solace.

"Stays crisp longer in the salty air," the sailor said, unwrapping the foil.

"Industrious," Poe said to himself.

At the Northern Hotel by the Cortland Street Ferry house, Poe loosened his shirt collar, glancing up at the gas lamp. He watched two ladies' silhouettes as they stopped to buy cut hyacinths. Through the steamy, smoky panes in the bow window, he saw the saloon was serving hot coffee, cakes, pies, confectionery, and fruit. The front door banged open to the racket of noisy sailors rendezvousing during layovers. As Poe entered through the crowd, and deafening noise, he ordered his regular, gulped down a hot cup of coffee and cornbread, took one bite and then engaged the proprietor. Poe pointed to a poster for Anderson's Solace Tobacco on the wall.

"Have you heard of John Anderson?" Poe asked.

"He is going to be our next mayor," the proprietor said.

"Is his name on the ticket?" Poe asked.

"I hear he is about to announce," the proprietor said.

Then Poe saw something out of the corner of his eye and pocketed the cornbread and exited to read the poster on the wall. Someone had scrawled an unintelligible graffiti on the poster reading: John Anderson's Havana Segar Store, 319 Broadway & Thompson.

Poe plunged on through a veil of motes that swirled up a shaft of light. He melted into a group of businessmen stopping nearby, who were conversing in English and German.

"The Benedict Building. It is the first cast iron front in New York City," an architect was carrying a blueprint, and explaining through a translator. Then Poe jerked back as he was just missed by the mad crush of omnibus carriages lumbering uptown from South Ferry. Servants, lugging hogsheads of sparkling water from the water pump, splatter water, which glimmered across the glazed cobblestones. Workmen nearby ripped down out-dated posters announcing the funeral of President William Henry Harrison, last April 10, 1841. They tore down the tattered shrouds of black drapery, so the gold ochre of daylight broke through.

Poe, disguised as Peasely, then stood outside Harrison's General Merchandise Store on Broadway and Prince Street, peering in at the cigars on display.

"Like what you see?" Gabriel Harrison came out to the street and invited Poe to come in. Once inside, he lifted the lid of a humidor of cigars, so Poe could breathe in their fragrance. Poe absorbed the scent of bags of snoose and unrolled tobacco leaves.

"These cigars remind me of the cigar girl who has

vanished," Poe said.

"Beautiful girls have to be wary," Harrison said.

"And has that hurt Mr. Anderson's business?" Poe said.

"You are missing the point. Sure Anderson is a businessman. He is a real estate genius. But he wants more," Harrison said.

"More cigars?" Poe said.

"Sure. And everyone knows he wants to be mayor," Harrison explained.

"Ambitious. What more could anyone want?" Poe said.

"Never mind," Harrison said. "Gabriel Harrison, proprietor."

"Peasely," Poe said. He sniffed a cigar. "Where did you get these cigars?"

"I run a legitimate business here," Harrison said.

"Are you implying Anderson is not?" Poe said.

"He wants to control the opium trade. That will give him

control of day and night. That is life. I do not know anything about the rest," Harrison said.

Poe looked at Harrison while taking a cigar. Harrison looked at him and lit his cigar. Poe looked away.

"I would like to find out if there is a life after death," Poe said. "And if there is, when do we get some time off?"

Poe walked the half-mile north to John Anderson's Havana Segar Store, 319 Broadway and Thompson and noticed the adjoining medical college and the hospital. He saw his reflection appearing in the window. He saw behind the glass, Havana coronas hutched by plugs of weed cud, shags of rope. He twisted the doorknob. Locked. He banged on the door. Peered in. Shadows. Still silence. Empty. He kicked the door, the glass rattled. He sat and taking the cornbread out of his pocket, he devoured it.

John Anderson was straining at his drudgework as sole proprietor. He unlocked the back door, laid out boxes of tobacco, unlocked the front door, then annoyed, he responded to a knock at the back door. He left the shadowy front of his store untended, the front door swung open, and its hinge creaking. There stood a deliveryman, juggling a cart of tobacco leaves.

Anderson paid the deliveryman and began off-loading the tobacco. Then he heard someone open the front door and walk inside.

"Who in the hell is this, now?" Anderson muttered.

"Snowden sent me," Poe said. He showed Anderson the clipping. "Edgar Allan Poe. A writer and an editor. And a poet."

"A poet?" Anderson said.

"Not as a purpose, but a passion," Poe explained.

"What might your obsession be?" Anderson asked.

"A thirst for a wilder Beauty than Earth supplies," Poe said.

"Let's hope your madness conveys supernatural powers," Anderson said. "I must keep my feet on the ground."

"What can you tell me about Mary Rogers?" Poe asked.

Anderson murmured to himself. Then he spoke directly.

"She disappeared, vanished," Anderson said.

"Now it's public information," Poe said.

Anderson looked around nervously and took Poe by the coat and locked the door. Neighbors come to the store windows and looked in him, then continued walking.

"I solve mysteries, with discretion," Poe said.

Anderson offered Poe a chair.

"Sit down," Anderson said. "Catch your breath."

A customer came to the door and then knocked, but Poe drew the shade.

"My stepfather imported Virginia tobacco to England," Poe said.

"It's a matter of social pressure. What does the public say about me?" Anderson said.

"They say you and the cigar girl couldn't be together and not be together any longer," Poe said.

"Oh, they're just jealous. You know how they gossip," Anderson said. "I will place three ads in Snowden's magazine if you can solve this mystery to my satisfaction."

"But there are too many misleading details in the news stories," Poe said. "Where should I begin?"

"She disappeared with a sailor once before," Anderson said.

"Who?" Poe asked.

"Named Philip Spencer," Anderson said. Then he recognized Poe's realization. "Right. The problem son of Secretary of War John Canfield Spencer."

"His family will hush up any scandal," Poe said.

Anderson sidled away, warily. Anderson took out a cigar wrapped in tin foil marked Anderson's Solace Tobacco and gave it to Poe. Poe slumped onto a bench and exhaled with a sigh.

"Something is missing. Something is overshadowing..." Poe started to say.

"All I know is what you write on paper," Anderson said. They exchange glances.

"How did you meet Spencer?" Poe asked.

"Last spring, when the Brig Somers docked here. He came

into my shop. Likes Partagas," Anderson said.

Poe eyed Anderson suspiciously, and then smiled warily. As Poe began to exit, they shook hands. A steam whistle blew as Poe disappeared into the bustling crowd.

11 ELYSIAN FIELDS

VENUS, A fading signal light, hung in the deepening blue over Elysian Fields in Hoboken, New Jersey. The sun sunk on the horizon, throwing a ray across the riverbank, transforming the shades of every gritty object. A cricket creaked. The inky clouds broke. The rain vanished.

On the other side of the river, near the Manhattan docks, an empty dory floated unmoored, scraping the shoreline, its finish chipped. The dory's sail had been ripped by the wind and gutted. A spider's hairy, matted brown body crawled over the canvas. Dead branches and leaves were sucked downstream. Sailors brought it in to shore with a grappling hook.

When Poe had moved to Philadelphia in May 1839, he was reborn, Edgar Allan Poe, Esq., although on the inside he was ravished, all but penniless. He started to re-cast himself through his fantasy life also by 1841 as Dupin *The Murders in the Rue Morgue*, his story using ratiocination. Poe re-invented himself as the rogue Le Chevalier César Auguste Dupin, a knight, whose honor was bestowed in the <u>Palais de la Légion d'Honneur</u> on the left bank of the <u>River Seine</u> in Paris.

Herein, as the author Poe, for the record, ostensibly to conceal his motives as a character called Dupin, used the task of solving a crime, to appear masked behind a false front. As you probably have assumed, in the version set in Paris, the fate of Mary Rogers would be told as if she were a Parisian grisette. The author followed, in minute detail, the essential, while merely paralleling the inessential, facts of the real murder of Mary Rogers. Thus all argument founded upon the fiction is applicable to the truth: and the investigation of the truth was the object.

The *Mystery* was composed by Edgar Allan Poe at a great distance from the scene of the atrocity, and with no other means of investigation than the newspapers afforded. Thus much escaped the writer of which he could have availed himself had he been upon the spot and visited the localities. The hypothetical details, by which that conclusion was attained, will be evident when you read on.

Poe was the lifeblood, the spiritual strength or *force d'âme* that drove the lure of the tale of ratiocination. The *femme fatale* enchanted him, mesmerically.

So, although he has been charged with cold-heartedly analyzing the murder, in cold blood, his numbness was crucial for finding the solution.

You should ask yourself, why my dearth of virtue *vis-à-vis* the dead girl? Why should Poe so resolutely exploit the mind of The Narrator and also the police?

You might consider Poe's aristocratic origins.

Poe felt the Narrator of his tale set in the Rue Morgue had worked as an oracle, guiding his mind to wander en route for Paris, where now in his imagination, he imagined storm clouds transforming into an unknown beauty's face above the River Seine, and below, on solid soil, he himself the *bête noire*, *écriture* in his modest library, *au secret* in a book closet on the third floor of No. 33 Rue Dunot, Fauborg Saint Germain.

On July 28, 1841, a long line formed around the water tap at Castle Point near Elysian Fields. The temperature was still extremely hot and muggy. Two men, the skeptical Henry Mallen of 333 Broadway, and his cynical friend, James W. Ballard of 321 Broadway, stood waiting in line to get a drink.

Mallen looked out onto the Hudson River just south of Elysian Fields. He saw an object floating 300 yards out from the west bank.

"Do you see a bundle of rags floating out there?" the Mallen asked.

"You mean in your imagination?" Ballard said.

"I mean about three hundred yards out," Mallen said.

"That is a mermaid who wants to take you home. First we will skin her, then we will roast her on a spit," Ballard said.

Mary Rogers's body floated underwater in an unreal glimmer, light severing the darkness in dribs and drabs. She murmured dreamily.

Then Mallen and Ballard slid a dinghy into the river. They

passed a red, ringing buoy. The sun was roasting them. A sailboat winged by at six knots. The buzz of cicadas faded and the sound of the water striking shore was fading in the distance, but the gulls cried and swooped overhead, their cries sinking like dead letters. The dinghy scraped a rock, and the oars strained.

Mallen peered over the side of the dinghy at the fish lurching below in the translucent green and at the murky kelp illuminated by rays of sun. Mallen craned back his head, drawing a bead on the horizon. He grunted, strong-arming the oars, his face grimacing against the pull, his eyes squinting. Mallen plowed deep furrows in the surface of the river. The air overhead was murky and still and thick.

Ballard felt sluggish, he shook his head, trying to clear it.

Mallen growled as the dinghy bucked. The water chopped. He winced as the oars scraped his hands. He skidded his hand across the surface, but that made the raw skin sore. His mouth was parched. The sunlight across the water was cut in zigzags.

Ballard anchored the boat and then dove in the water and came up fighting the current, spitting out water and treading toward the body. He reached the buoyant package and wrestled it to the dinghy.

"Jesus," Mallen said as he touched her hand.

Ballard sunk back, closing his eyes. He was winded and dripping anxious sweat. He rubbed his face with his raw palms and wrung his hands. He struggled to calm himself, his jaw grinding. Mallen felt the current sweeping cold and deep below him, pulling the body away. He dove under her body and paddled like a crab, dragging her back to the boat. He boosted her up into the boat, which lurched as he dropped her in. Then he threw his leg up and pitched himself inside.

Then Ballard was sick. He shoveled a handful of water and washed off his face and sat upright and stiff and looking at the horizon, he pulled up the anchor and turned the boat around. He sucked bitterness through his teeth. He heard the clanging of the buoy-bell.

"Let us call this deliverance," Mallen said.

12 POE DISCOVERS HER MURDERED

POE AND Tibbs got word of the discovery when a breathless
Carman delivered an editor to the paper. Poe and Tibbs threw
down their cards and were pushed off by the next ferry from Manhattan toward Elysian Fields. As they pulled closer to the
shoreline, near Castle Point, they could see a crowd gathered on
the dock. Poe watched the skeptic and the cynic hoisting up a body
tied in a bundle.

Poe saw Mary Rogers's beautiful torso turning in a torn
blue dress. Her seductive legs were dressed in stockings and
garters. She was stretched out on her side.

When the ferry docked, Poe and Tibbs walked to the body.
Poe grasped her arm to ease her into a restful position. One
onlooker held Poe back by his shoulders.

Poe tried to untie her hands but the rope was wet.
He rolled her onto her back tenderly, caressing her soft
hand. Mary Rogers rolled over dreamily. Poe sucked in
his breath. Mary Rogers's face had been butchered to a

mummy. The onlookers covered their faces. Mary Rogers's wet body was bloated from taking in water. The onlookers murmured.

"Murder!" a loudmouth said.

Poe kneeled down beside her body and held her swollen hands, examining them.

Then a leatherhead appeared in the crowd, regarding Poe suspiciously.

"Who are you?" the leatherhead asked Poe. Poe was distant and preoccupied.

"Shake from her this trash in which she was embedded," Poe said.

The leatherhead regarded Poe's worn old army boots.

"Here, soldier," the leatherhead, said.

Poe looked askance at the leatherhead.

"Soldier of Fortune, then," the leatherhead said. "Help me."

The autopsy on Mary Rogers was held in Hoboken in Hudson County, N.J. on the night of July 28, 1841. Dr. Richard F. Cook, the county coroner, made the examination with his own hands and his own eyes, by first removing the clothes from Mary Rogers's body, and unwinding some loose jute.

"No attachments," Dr. Cook said, matter-of-factly. "No rings. No jewelry. Buried in the flesh of her throat is a strip of lace trimming, which was torn from her dress, see? Bound tightly here, in the flesh of her neck." Dr. Cook struggled to free it, but his fingers were entangled. "That was the cause of death. Strangulation."

"What is this around her waist?" Poe asked.

"It looks like strings," Dr. Cook said. "Maybe from her bonnet. Were twined around here and secured by a kind of hitch in the back."

"No lady tied that knot," Poe said.

"No. It is a slipknot," Dr. Cook said.

"A sailor's knot. I wonder if a sailor got her pregnant?"

Poe said.

"There is not the slightest trace of pregnancy. There is evidence of sexual intercourse. Many times," Dr. Cook explained.

"Rape?" Poe asked.

"Yes," Dr. Cook said.

"Tied and gagged and raped and strangled and thrown into the river," Poe said.

"Put her body in a temporary grave until we can have the inquest," Dr. Cook said to the workmen sitting outside. The crew of workmen struggled in the heat to place Mary's body in an oblong box.

"They don't even know for sure who this one was," the gravedigger said. They were all sweating with effort. They lowered Mary Roger's body into a bed of salt and then lowered her into a coffin and put the coffin into another larger box of salt. They then slipped her body under the dark boathouse.

Across the bay that night, the air was muggy again even after the rain. The water was gray and rough. A red beacon bobbed. The water surged. Anderson saw Poe step off the bobbing ferry onto Manhattan.

"Are you back for business or pleasure?" Anderson asked Poe with the cordiality of familiar strangers.

"For the fresh air," Poe said.

"Oh, the air is free," Anderson said. "Breathe easy."

Poe had seen Anderson pacing up and down. Poe had thought at first that he was impatiently waiting for someone to arrive. But then Anderson walked into the city with Poe.

"Have you heard that Mary Rogers was discovered?" Poe said.

"No," Anderson said. He did not smile.

"I just saw her," Poe said.

Anderson did not say anything then, but he touched his beard self-consciously.

"I am sorry," Poe said. "Mary Rogers is dead."

"Come to my shop with me," Anderson said. "We can talk

there."

First the fluttering of the sails and the sounds of the dock faded away into haze. Poe smelled the salty air giving away to the grunge of the city streets. Anderson was chewing a cigar and he seemed weary from fighting something. He bit off a nibble of the cigar and spit it out. Beyond the end of the dock the waves rolled toward the bay. Poe felt Anderson staring at him with his owl-like and remote eyes. Then Poe was seduced by the romance of the city the exotic warmth of the street cafes. Poe wondered if this was part of Anderson's web, knowing everyone, a familiar face, and a power.

Then when they got to Anderson's Segar store, Anderson brought Poe back into his private, serenely pleasurable and opulent mahogany office. Poe brushed the fertile, bold forms of lush garden plants, with intense shafts of sunlight knifing through the porthole-style windows. Poe could feel the nearness of the shimmering ecstatic seascape beyond. Poe wondered, what is personal here? What is private and what is public? What is reality and what is intrigue in this setting? The essence of this milieu is artifice.

Poe recalled the murder scene at the dock in New Jersey, the stark daytime, gray sky, no rain, a skiff, its sails ripped by wind and whipped by rain, then beached and gutted. The matted stringers of weeds. The body of Mary Rogers lying on the beach, her mouth clogged with lather. A brown spider crawling in the boat, through the last bubbles of rainfall.

Then Anderson tossed his cigar into the fireplace in anger. Poe dropped onto the couch. As Anderson went to the storefront to take care of some business, Poe fell into a restless sleep, with Muddie's lullabies and dead branches and leaves peeled off and sucked away, green phosphorous on the rims of the waves as they break, and Poe floating underwater in the unreal glimmer of the bay.

The Poe heard the percussive rhythm of Anderson's boots wood floors echoing against the silence. Anderson was looking down his nose at Poe, directing his hollow glance and a flashy smile toward him.

"I think your story could have more about the cigar shop,"

Anderson said. Poe started to wriggle uneasily. "My career has been one run after another," Anderson said. "I am always running for something. You think I am the most useful man for you to know."

"You want my insider's information from the press," Poe said.

"I do not mind if the press examines me," Anderson said. I have lived an ethical life. And a well spent life."

"You are free to choose for yourself," Poe said. He could see Anderson's dignified, aristocratic background, from a rich boy's club, and though he was long past grown, he was still sowing wild oats. Everything with Anderson was a negotiation or a poker game. Poe wondered what social programs of Anderson's might turn against Poe's nature. Poe looked down at Anderson's boots and saw a dusting of clay. "As I am."

"I was not free when the stock market crashed," Anderson said. "The world was dizzy. I had the feeling that something frightening was happening. The air on the trading floor was so still that it seemed thick, as if the world was afraid of the heights, and was sluggishly trying to balance, but was reeling and could not clear its head. But there I was in the middle of the plunge, thinking, When this is over, what am I going to do, I have to stand pat, I can not just bail out or I will not have anything to fight with. I never went wrong aiming for rightness. I am good at gambling, any kind of gambling. Even on people, like you.

"I like a good fight," Anderson explained. "I like the notoriety, it is good for me. I am a warrior who fights other men for personal power, never mind the cause. That is why I have no fear of death. I am only fearful of failing and getting trapped under someone else's thumb. I used to see in college that it was just a haven for crumbling faith, with its old-fashioned resources. I thought if I sit here and argue over these issues, I would end up broke.

"When I drink at the cocktail hour or thereabouts my annoyances wash away with the tide," Anderson said. "Then the answers always come to me."

Anderson worked his fingers through his hair, and tapped out mental notes on the tips of his fingers.

Poe could see Tibbs knocking at the front door.

"Blood-thirsty newshounds," Anderson said. "You are not some ordinary scandalmonger," Anderson said sarcastically to Poe.

"Those demons are the best reason to keep on, if just to spite them," Poe said.

"These news-hounds are, paranoid, fragmented," Anderson said. "My viability as a human being will make them look like a shroud." Then Anderson shouted to the newshounds. "You think you can twist everything. You think you can make me sweat. Here, put on my hat, at least cover your horns, and your tails, and do not forget your hooves!"

"Have you decided against running for mayor?" Poe asked.

"I will not be forced out of public office by someone who murdered Mary Rogers to get back at me. Rumors! You can tell them to write that I will contribute to the reward being offered for catching the killer of Mary Rogers."

13 RELY ON YOUR NERVE

ON THE night of August 11, 1841, the acting coroner, Presiding Justice Gilbert Merritt of Hudson County, New Jersey came in from fishing with Acting Mayor of Manhattan Elijah Purdy.

"Exhume Mary Rogers' body from this temporary grave in Hoboken," Purdy said to Justice Merritt.

"The condition of her body prevents inspection," Justice Merritt said. He handed Purdy a swatch of Mary's dress, the flowers from out of Mary's hat, one of her garters, the bottom of her pantolette, a shoe, and a lock of her hair.

"Use these fragments for positive identification," Justice Merritt said to Purdy. "Was she married?"

"No," Purdy said.

"I want positive identification by her family," Justice Merritt said.

"She has a mother," Purdy said.

"Take the evidence to her mother, then, for a positive

identification," Justice Merritt said. "Is there any place in Manhattan where you can inter the body?"

"Behind the West Presbyterian Church at the north terminus of Varick Street," Purdy said.

When the last Hoboken Ferry was loaded that night, Purdy and Carman Boyce hoisted Mary Rogers's body and coffin over their shoulders and hoisted it on.

"Hurry, boys!" the ferryman said, shoving off toward Manhattan.

Boyce plunked down the ungainly coffin, catching his breath.

"The body was not Mary Rogers's," the rumormongers whispered under the steam.

When Carman Boyce arrived at the medical college on Crosby Street in Manhattan, he drove his wagon to the dock and then off-loaded a gunnysack containing Mary Rogers's dead body and handed it down to a medical student.

The Carman said, "I was not present when the body was

taken out of the box at the dead house. I know the box was taken out of the starboard hatch. I sat on the box while driving it to the dead house. There was a cloth over it. There was chloride of lime all around it."

"Right," the medical student said. He handed Boyce the money.

Phoebe Rogers stood alone at 144 Pitt in Manhattan on the morning of August 12, 1841. She hovered over the stove with an egg in her hand. She heard the front door pushed open, and when she saw Purdy and his officious manner, she dropped the egg. It broke, but she picked it up and tried to hold it together. She froze as Purdy laid down the items of Mary Rogers's clothing on the cabinet in front of Phoebe Rogers.

As Purdy stood, waiting for Rogers's response, he absent-mindedly opened a humidor, but found it empty.

Phoebe Rogers picked up the lock of her daughter's hair and brushed it across her cheek. She hummed "The itsy-bitsy spider," to herself.

At the funeral home that night, Poe sat with Phoebe Rogers by Mary Rogers's closed casket.

"I do not want any company," Phoebe Rogers said apathetically. Then Anderson joined them.

"I could not sleep," Anderson said, apologetically.

"Clock kept going just the same," Poe said.

"You wore your suit," Anderson said, his voice faint, as he brushed off Poe's shoulder.

"I am tired," Phoebe Rogers said.

"She does not have to suffer anymore," Anderson said.

"Finish up, it is time to go," the mortician said.

"You go home and get some rest now," Poe said to Phoebe Rogers. He helped her stand up and walked her out the door.

Anderson paid the mortician.

"Always a pleasure to see you..." Anderson said to the mortician. "...Go."

Poe and Anderson then stayed and Anderson dealt Poe and

Mary Rogers a hand of cards.

"I want to put a ring on her hand," Anderson said, his voice melancholy.

But when Poe opened the casket, it was empty.

At the Presbyterian Church funeral, the red-faced minster led the procession to the altar through this narrow church. Poe and Anderson led the pallbearers.

"Easy come, easy go," Anderson muttered to himself. As Anderson shifted the weight of the coffin, Poe reached for the pew, but tore off a strand of black crepe. Phoebe Rogers sat alone.

"We are not going to hang you," a leatherhead's voice muttered to Poe. "Not for very long anyway."

"Do you want to know why you are here?" the minister said. "You are here to salt this earth. Not as some secret seasoning, but so God's flavor can be tasted and savored. Because, if life loses its flavor, it is good for nothing: throw it out in the street, it is useless."

After the ceremony, while the hearse was rocking to the

West Presbyterian Cemetery, some strangers stopped to watch. The driver parked down in the corner of the cemetery by a green tent standing under a bare oak. The coffin was placed there, supported by rails above the grave. The scant wind rattled the tent.

"I envy Mary Rogers," Anderson said. "I want to be with her. There is blood on the moon. Like the end of the world."

"Rely on your nerve," Poe said. "That is the only thing that keeps us in the here and now."

14 POE IN THE HOUSE OF HATE

AT THE Halls of Justice, the prison called the Tombs, the building, which was designed after an ancient mausoleum, stood harsh, bleak, cold and damp.

A leatherhead rubbed his nose against his prisoner's, which was shackled to the floor. He bashed the suspect's head against the wall.

"I can not hear you!" the leatherhead said. Then he told the jailers, "Jerk him to Jesus."

A night watchman came through the door then.

"Mr. Anderson to see you, sir," the night watchman said.

The leatherhead shoved the suspect inside the jail and slammed the door shut, and wiped off his hands. The leatherhead then closed the door with a rigid sense of decorum.

"Sorry about these questions, Sir. They are just a formality. We do not want to injure your reputation," the leatherhead said.

Anderson nodded, as the Leatherhead showed him out the

front door.

"Discharged for lack of evidence," the leatherhead said to the clerk.

Anderson walked out. There on the corner stood Poe. They walked together. Anderson looked over toward Mary Rogers' house as they walked by.

"Damn that house of hate. That place drove me out of politics," Anderson said.

The leatherhead stood plastering wanted posters on the brick wall.

At the Northern Hotel by the Cortland Street Ferry House, that night, Poe looked in on the bow window and saw a waiter cleaning up for the night and flipping chairs over and setting them on the tables. He overhead more rumormongers exiting.

"Mary Rogers is still alive," One of them said. "Mary was a suicide. Anderson..." said the other.

Then one shushed the other and pointed toward Poe, in-dicating he was a nosy outsider.

In the dead shadows under the trees, there was something dripping down like black spackle and there were women hookers flitting and ambling in one motion like bats. One of them had an injured foot. An accommodating and permissive old gentleman pimp accompanied her. He had white hair, and might have been the toastmaster in a social club, so innocuous and neighborly was his appearance. His hooker had red hair and freckles. They would have looked just right at the opera, watching the main event. One of the other pimps near him bore a stark-staring resemblance to his own hooker. They both had their black hair parted down the middle and they were both built thin and rangy like hill country people. Their profiles were dropforged like the same dull penny.

Poe was walking toward them when he saw a gang of big beefeaters was steamed up on the corner gawking, sizzling with gristle till their fluffy coats could have come unyoked. The steak-eaters started giving the country hooker a hard time, and she was flaunting her crotch and saying, "Here mister, who gets the wishbone?" About fifteen steps behind her was her pimp. He slinked by Poe, coming the other way, his hands working the change in his pockets, and he had the strangest smirk on his face.

He had on a simpering laugh, and he nodded his head as he passed

the steak-eaters, as said to them, "Yes, you sure know how to call

them, mister." Poe thought, that hooker is that pimp's sister, and

that old gentleman is that limping girl's father. Her family was

crooked, and perverted, and love was dirty and crippled. We do

not treat our kind like a necessary evil; we do not sell our children.

The city did this. Poe heard the sound of someone following him

home, but he hurried on.

That was when Poe ran into the leatherhead.

"Poe," the leatherhead said. "You knew Mary Rogers from

before, did you not?'

"From the smoke shop," Poe said.

"She will be better off," the leatherhead said. "This will

give her a chance to get away from the drugs, to get off the

streets."

Poe knew the leatherhead had been trained to say all the

right things. Poe wondered why he was so suspicious of

everyone's motives. Maybe it was the leatherhead's cool professionalism. It seemed like everything had been rehearsed. But what is wrong with that? I am glad when someone is cool and professional when the time comes.

"Would you like a shot of peace of mind?' the leatherhead offered Poe a drink of whiskey.

"Unction for my soul," Poe said.

"After nine o'clock. I have to go to the courthouse," the leatherhead said.

"Goodbye," Poe said.

"You individual," the leatherhead said. "I heard you are a womanizer."

"You hear a lot of things about me I will bet," Poe said.

"A rusty one, I heard," the leatherhead said. "What are you looking at?" Poe noticed the leatherhead was extremely pale and his eyes were darting around the streets. Poe knew his own imagination was wound tight.

Poe stood in the alley behind John Anderson's Segar Store

and knocked on the back door. Anderson was surprised to see Poe, but he welcomed him. Anderson seemed shell-shocked.

"Time and tide can change so quickly," Anderson said. Anderson rubbed in passing a japanned chest with brush-strokes used to imitate enameling, two prints of Chinese ports, plus silk wallpaper. He pulled a frosted glass out of the icebox and poured in bourbon and a spoonful of sugar and crushed mint leaves and shaved ice. "Julep?"

"Less than lethal, sir," Poe said.

"I have heard you are a southern gentleman," Anderson said.

"From Richmond, sir, where we drink our juleps in the morning," Poe said. "Spencer is in the Tombs."

"Speaking of demons," Anderson said. "Slavery to public opinion is too high a price to pay for success."

Anderson looked idly at the music-box, cranked it and it began to play "Norma." He started cleaning up his space on the desk, straightening out and setting things in order. "Ask Spencer" Anderson said.

"I thought you were like a bank, too big to fail," Poe said.

"Because everybody put Mary Rogers up on a pedestal," Anderson said. "She was only shackled to me by conscience. I suppose one day you might be the one to drag me down, too, and leave my clay feet exposed. What do the reporters say?"

"They say you use people," Poe said.

"Why do you act as if words are stronger than actions?" Anderson said.

"That keeps my enemies nebulous," Poe said. The chimes on the clock struck 9:30. "Isn't life grand?"

"What is the alternative?" Anderson said.

Poe loved double meanings. And so, now that his ambiguous marriage had cracked his personality to shards, Poe had retreated to a brooding romantic, wandering the docks. Poe had always found himself seeking rivals like Anderson to work with. He had walked by Anderson's shop before; he had been allured to Mary Rogers in the day. At night, however, Poe struggled to stay clear of opium and write. Poe had always slipped under the cloak of night to gamble and live out his dreams but now he had a story to tell.

Because Poe's mind was in a racket at home, with his wife and his mother-in-law and the boarders, because Poe was excitable, dreamy and hot-tempered himself, he found himself writing in a style that was singularly pure and idiomatic with a nervous clearness. He hoped to force his idea of order on his world that was sailing out of control.

Is Anderson trolling me in, or is this a deep-rooted mystery? Poe wondered. If I want to find the answers, I will have to overcome the barrier of physical distance, beat my personal antagonists, the competitive writers, ignore the mystic force of my dead father, who may have gone up in flames, maybe even overcome my own personality, which is moody and susceptible to drinking binges, and of course, I will have to ignore the tuberculosis which killed my mother and father, which is destroying my wife and will someday, perhaps inevitably... Is it any wonder I am a melancholy, haunted man. At least I find what terrible beauty there is. Tormented or not, I am still a newshound at heart, drawn to the godforsaken, shameless newspaper form. If I can only solve the shocking murder and violation of Mary Rogers by my own singular method, my own ratiocination, I will make a name for myself.

Poe felt homesick and trapped in Manhattan now.

"Let us take off our coats and play a game of chess," Anderson proposed. He was dressed in a vest and a shirt but no jacket and his hair was slicked back with rosemary hair lotion. Poe murmured as he played a game of chess with Anderson.

Poe's pawn reached the last row of the enemy, and the white exchanged his pawn for the black queen.

"My king is liberating your queen," Poe said.

"Checkmate," Anderson said. Then he whistled through his teeth: ts-s-s, but too late as a cat jumped up on the board and started to knock down all the players. Poe brushed all the pieces and the cat off the board, onto the floor. Poe took a cup of beer and prepared to toss it into the cat's face, but thought twice and then drank it down.

"Mary Cecilia Rogers lived a public life as common as a dust mote, wedged behind the counter, selling plugs of weed cud and shags of rope, bags of snoose or cigar boxes with Havana coronas hutched inside like rolled fume," Poe said. "She served the big-spenders who drew baccarat and the penny-ante newspaper types alike."

"It takes all kinds," Anderson said.

"She died alone," Poe said.

"You are drunk," Anderson said.

"Maybe her death will wake up public opinion and force political change," Poe said. "Maybe her death will help transform law enforcement in Manhattan."

"It is only sensational," Anderson said. "It is just another excuse for stirring people up. That is the American way."

Poe imagined her decomposing body pitching over and lurching to the surface of the murmuring Hudson River.

"The light from the lurid gulf was a sinister and fitting

grave, ringed with trees dark in color and mournful in form and attitude, wreathing themselves into sad, solemn and spectral shapes that conveyed ideas of mortal sorrow and untimely death," Poe said to himself.

"Stop now," Anderson said.

"It is just talk," Poe said.

"Two-penny papers," Anderson said with disgust. Rumormongers and rubarbmongers and busybodies..."

"She had a life like yours and mine, you know," Poe said.

"Do you have to take everything so personally?" Anderson said.

"Was she killed on the New Jersey side or the Manhattan side? If she was killed in New Jersey, why should walking out in the country be taking a chance for her?" Poe said. "All kinds of people were there. She was a friend of yours."

"Maybe the killers were making her a scapegoat for public apathy about crime," Anderson said.

"The leatherheads and the Night watch?" Poe said.

"Leatherheads," Anderson said in disgust. "Unarmed, dressed in street clothes. Two constables from each city ward and six marshals. The Night Watch: one hundred and forty-six men, who work regular jobs during daylight. Street crime is overrunning Manhattan."

"We need full investigation and complete reform of the police system," Poe said. "There are twenty thousand people living in Manhattan now."

"Why would you choose to work on a mystery so deep and perplexing?" Anderson asked. "Because you think you are some detective?"

"To clear your good name," Poe said. "Maybe the spectral water images have resonated in my twisted imagination. Perhaps my vanity just got the best of me. Perhaps it is to prod the investigation. Really it is to direct inquiry."

"You cynic," Anderson said.

"Do not forget, the hunter of small things," Poe said. "What did you expect me to write about? Have you seen these extras in banner headlines on cheap paper stock coming out to cover steamship arrivals bringing two-week-old news from Europe? I have a craving for the real news."

"It is becoming catching on contact," Anderson said.

"I am up at five a.m., pulling the coat of every merchant before three p.m.," Poe said. "There is a clipper ship bobbing off of Montauk to grab European newspapers first, there are steam locomotive racing west across Long Island to get out extras. Why not us, writing about our neighborhood, our friends."

"I heard you called a speculating man," Anderson said.

"Did you hear that Mary Rogers had disappeared once before, on October 5, 1838, leaving behind a suicide note for her mother?" Poe said. "She apparently ran off with a sailor. Maybe it was Spencer, but it did not work out. They stayed in Hoboken that time.

"I also heard that on Sunday, July 25, 1841, Mary Rogers knocked on the door of a tenant at her mother's house, who was also her fiancée, Daniel Payne, as he was making his toilet," Poe said. "She said that she was off to visit her aunt, Mrs. Downey. That evening, there was a violent thunderstorm, with prevalent north and northeast winds, which began before sundown, and cleared away after ten p.m. There was a powerful current running downriver, striking at Glass House Point."

"No Christian will ever relax in the holy excitement, till the foul perpetrators be discovered and brought to justice," Anderson read from the paper.

"You know Daniel Payne's body was found near the site of Mary Rogers' death, with a suicide note," Poe said. "He had taken laudanum."

"Well, does that solve the crime then?" Anderson said.

"No, because I am not just a taleteller," Poe said. "In this case I am a fact finder. I may be steeped in his sense of romance, but this is not just an ambiguous and enigmatic riddle. It was not Payne that dissipated prodigal. Maybe it is just my vanity, that makes me believe I can purify some part of Manhattan by solving this mystery which has riddled my rummy rivals."

"You are pursuing this crime with a vengeance," Anderson said.

Poe appeared transformed by the depths of his feelings. Anderson saw the intense sense of loss, though Poe had always seemed remote. Poe seemed to read Anderson's mind.

"Women," Poe said. "My mother was never more than a face on a card. Then my nurse-maid, serving me gin-toast and laudanum and lip-service. My child bride on her ivory pedestal, my muse. The cigar girl, transformed into an arabesque of smoke. Is this some strange universal that defines me? How can I change?"

"Death is always news," Anderson said. "Where do you live, by the way?"

"In a tenement at 195 East Broadway," Poe said. "In a garret under the eaves, but I work in a spacious study one floor below."

"And what is your stock?" Anderson said. They were both drinking now.

"I am the son of two actors, Elizabeth Arnold Poe, one of the handsomest women in America, and David Poe, Jr. They were always touring. I was told they were erratic, dramatic, and somewhat vain." Poe took out a miniature watercolor portrait of his mother from his briefcase. Anderson looked at it. Poe took it back and saw a woman dressed in an Empire waisted gown and a ribboned bonnet, with curly, dark hair plummeting out to her shoulders. The painting was done in a mannered, superficial, heavily ornamented style. She was shown wearing enormous pearl earrings. Her eyes were pictured as cat-like, and dark, and enlarged in a mournful way like a big-eyed cheap greeting card.

"I was raised by John Allan, a merchant," Poe continued. When I was young, I wanted to prove I was a better swimmer than Byron, so I swam six miles in the James River."

"I heard you were a pretty wild young man," Anderson said.

"I was blistered by the sun once swimming all day," Poe said nodding. He wished he were there now.

In the Tombs that August night, Poe walked up to the

leatherhead sitting behind the front desk of the city jail.

"Are you holding Midshipman Philip Spencer?" Poe asked.

"Let us see, Spencer. Do you mean the nephew of Secretary of War J. C. Spencer and Judge Ambrose Spencer, New York politician?" the jailer asked.

"I want to talk to him," Poe said.

"There is a press blackout on the Mary Rogers case," the jailer explained.

Then Poe bribed the leatherhead.

"I want to talk to him for background on a story about privateering," Poe said. "This is off the record."

"You have got five minutes," the jailer said.

As Poe met Spencer for the first time, face-to-face, Spencer was suspicious.

"Did you make a deal with Anderson?" Poe asked Spencer.

Spencer gazed searchingly into Poe's eyes and rubbed his fingers together, smelling them and closed his eyes dreamily. Poe then slipped Spencer his own vial of laudanum. Spencer then nodded yes, and drank it and relaxed.

"I am paying for a murder someone else committed," Spencer said. "When my uncle hears about this, he will get me out of here."

"Were you and Mary Rogers's brother sailing together on the same ship?" Poe asked.

Spencer then called out for the guard by rattling the door of the jail.

Poe walked out of the lyceum lecture he had just given and lit a cigar and drew in the fragrant sot-weed like a furnace as he walked through his shadow world. Each time he inhaled, the contour of his dark form sharpened against the deep background. In this night world his shadow walked like a ghost, blurring into the dark around him. The spark and the glow of his smoking showed Poe's forehead, which stood out and the hollows of his eyes were sucked in, sculpted to see, not to express.

Poe sought the light of the gas lamps and followed the

black smell of coffee. His jaw worked against itself as the stream

of American blurb sunk around him and into his negative night.

Anywhere out of this world: Poe was a body between places and

times, with fascinated eyes that gazed into the dark sea of night at

the underneath the world. Poe's smoke interwove in crossing

currents, his reflection rippled on the glass and the glass breathed

him in and out like a magic show: a puff of smoke, a flash of light.

The illusions multiplied as doors opened, and as pedestrians

flowed away.

Magic world that spun around him, pulling birds from the

air and dissolving them into the trees. Poe walked past Browning

& Durnham's North River Foundry and locomotive engine shop on

North Moore and the Hudson River, and he saw New Jersey drift

away in the distance. Poe seemed to drift too, but he was sear-

ching for evidence.

Poe's feet floated on the dark ground and waited for the

blurry horse-drawn cars of the New York & Harlem Railroad,

which sauntered past every half-hour.

"Whose melodious voice is that?" Poe heard a signalman

say to a redcap.

"I heard Mary Rogers ... " the redcap started to say.

"You told me that story, dammit," the signalman said. "I am sick of it."

"I tried to get one large toolbox," the redcap said.

"Good," the signalman said.

"I put lots of money in it," the redcap said.

"You could head home now," the signalman said. "What time did you start?"

"5:30," the redcap said. "I can not remember anything."

"That is not your train," the signalman said.

The train passed by but no one got on. Two men got off.

"How did you read my mind?" the redcap said.

"I saw you looking at the train, Am I supposed to be there?" the signalman said.

"Do not tell the leatherhead I said this. He does not know," the redcap said.

"You will let me know about that in the morning," the signalman said.

"I found out Mary Rogers left from here that day she was murdered with Mr. Anderson, the seegar storekeeper," the redcap said.

"I wondered why you had that big smile on," the signalman said. "Take it easy." He quieted the redcap then. The signalman turned to Poe and smiled.

One other man stood at the stop. Then Poe heard the distant clanging of the bell and he heard the sound of the train wheels braking and the huffing of the horse. Then he saw the train slowing and braking. Then the car stopped and Poe saw the conductor swing himself off the train. He was mustached. His cap read: New York & Harlem, Assistant Conductor. Poe climbed on and took a seat and Manhattan seemed different now and Anderson seemed different now, too.

Poe embodied his own shadow. His face was shaded with by the darkness of Mary Rogers's murder. She had been abandoned to oblivion.

Two blackbirds in the street bit at each other. Their claws zipped together, their beaks itching at each other's throats.

Her own excessively romantic, free-wheeling nature. Her mother had mistrusted her intentions. She was like a firefly with her brilliant, short life.

Poe smelled opium smoke, foggy, misty, nebulous, and hazy.

15 POE'S UNCERTAIN LIFE

THAT WICKED hot summer Muddie, who had once been forgiving and flexible as a mimosa, began clinging to positives, because their lives were so uncertain. She would sing songs by Stephen Foster to soothe Sissy. Muddie's eyes became clearer now, but more brittle. Muddie and Poe rocked back and forth like a see-saw every morning at breakfast.

"I am sick of your drinking," Muddie whispered. And Poe would explain the practice in Richmond. Poe's drink was his anesthetic. He was childish about it, and it made him happy in the morning, as if he were hosting a party.

"You can not have a party every morning," Muddie said. "You can not go to work with the reek of alcohol on your breath. You will drag everybody's mood down with you. It is a battle for me to get anything done around this boarding house already." Muddie had been simmering, trying to think of what she could say to wake him up, but nothing she could think of would work. "If you do not have the backbone to be the father in this house, then I will have to do it, and I will. No more drinking in here."

"It is no problem," Poe said. Sissy sat at the kitchen table, constructing a bridge from pipe cleaners. Poe was dressed for work, smelling like iron and bay rum and hard liquor. His jaw was tense. His eyes were beat. Muddie was slipping around behind them, getting lunch ready. She was fuming. Sissy was trying to read her father's mind. But it was hard. He was mad. But he was not mad all the time. This was worse. This time he was not showing anything. This time he poured himself a cup of coffee in a blue carnival glass cup and sat across the kitchen table from Sissy. He did not say anything for a long time. Sissy did not say anything. Muddie turned over the timer and Sissy watched the sand trickle down.

"Hickory-dickory-dock," Sissy said. "The sand ran down the clock.

"Your Mother said you ran off from school," Poe said. "Why?" Sissy looked down at her hands and watched her fingers kneading. "When are you going to get your feet on the ground?" Sissy had never heard that expression before. She looked down at her feet. "We all have to go to school," Poe said, with his grim patience. "When I was your age I went to school. When your mother was your age she went to school. Now it's time for you and all the other kids your age to go to school. The other kids have to get up at six-forty-five in the morning. You do too. They have to put their clothes on. You do too. They have to eat their oats. You do too. They have to go to school. You do too. When school is over they come home. That is the way it is. That is the way it has always been. I do not make the rules." Poe stared across at her, demanding an answer.

Sissy was lost.

"If I could just get back home to Richmond," Sissy said. Poe's eyes sagged with grieving. She could never reach up to his hands, the fists of a warhorse, or make him smile, his mustache was prickly and rough and his poker-face hung like a mask of scorn.

"You really think you will get away with this," Poe told Muddie. "It's written all over her face."

Home felt unreal to Sissy, as if a puppeteer had drawn up

her strings but left her dangling above everyone else. Her chest was choked.

"Please do not drink anymore at breakfast," Sissy said. Then Muddie dropped a glass. She picked up the broken shards of glass as Poe stormed out the door.

Because the Saturday morning rush of customers had already begun at Poe's favorite breakfast nook, the families were gathered outside. The sunlight's rays of color were bleaching the surface of the ground into crystals. Beard grass jumped out of the dirt, the silent grindstone of nature. Steam rose at the counter. Newspaper racks on the sidewalk had all the same news: murder. Poe stopped and read the activities posted at the entrance: auction, dance, and smudged business cards.

Poe breezed through the doorway with familiarity, nodding at familiar strangers shuffling by like the masks on a deck of cards. He paused at the entrance, inhaled the sweet smell of breakfast time: link sausage and French toast and watered-down coffee. The flavor was as easy-going as the glad-handing familiarity.

"Well, how in the world are you this morning?" Sarah

asked Poe. He tried to grasp her around the waist, but she skirted out of his grip. Poe sat down alone at a table, surrounded by strangers.

"It is a good thing you are still paying attention anyway," Sarah looked back at Poe and winked.

"Coffee would do me some good," Poe said. Sarah poured him a cup and told him to serve himself at the buffet. He loaded his plate, returned and sat down. Then Poe imagined Mary Rogers sitting across from him at the table while he was the killer preparing to make the kill.

"You see we can get along just fine," Mary Rogers whispers in her killer's ear. "You have got me."

"Is this what we wanted?" the killer said. He was in the mood for something different. "I am changing."

"Well, what do you want?" Mary Rogers asked. "Fried grasshopper?"

"We have all eaten grasshoppers," the killer said. "In bread. When they combine the wheat, grasshoppers jump in."

"Thank you for telling me that," Mary Rogers said. "Why is it always so tempting to steal?" Then she took the syrup from her killer.

When the door to the kitchen opened, the racket erupted from dish washing and plates clanking and water spraying.

"Gesund heit," Mary Rogers said.

"How do you feel?" the killer asked her.

"I thought you were terrified of the little demon," Mary Rogers said.

"Tell me," the killer said.

"He is a little invisible speck so far," Mary Rogers said. "All he wants is to be real like you."

Poe imagined his nerves were strained.

"I remember when I was a little girl," Mary Rogers said. She laughed. "My father used to take me out and order a drink for me. It was such a feeling of power." She pinched the bridge of her nose.

"You have a headache," Anderson said.

"Yes," Mary Rogers said. Poe imagined their struggle was the backbone of all the action. "It is a shame you do not have faith in me."

"Your headache is gone, is it? I know, because I've got it now," Anderson said.

How does a man raise a son? Poe wondered. Right words: honor, courage, and beauty. But what force can right words have in such a dark day in such a dark year. But then he stepped outside the restaurant and he could hear the clang and pull of the ships. The world around him clanged, inflamed with life. Poe imagined Anderson and Mary Rogers talking to each other as they walked through here together.

"You smell like my Dad," Mary Anderson said. "Like cigars." Anderson knew her kind of flirting. He saw her feminine form had changed. Anderson bluffed Mary Rogers then, tougher and more experienced in matters of love but hiding his fear that he would become entangled with her. So he hid any love he felt for her and appeared uninterested. Mary Rogers watched the expression on his face, as he was thinking, its signs of struggle, and its revelation of love like worry.

"I want to become more open to you," Mary Rogers said. "We have come this far together."

Poe knew Anderson was a man who had to take action, or he would feel nothing. A porter moved someone's luggage down from the hotel and Poe remembered his dream that morning.

Poe had been crawling through an enormous tunnel. He arrived at Mary Rogers's door. He knocked and then realized he had brought no luggage. Poe could sees Mary Rogers inside watching him and talking to someone about something she had done wrong. Then Mary Rogers walked to the door. Do you love me? Mary Rogers had asked Poe. Then rain poured down in sheets and flooded the island.

16 *THE SIGN OF THE CROW*

POE WALKED into *The Sign of the* Crow, a Hoboken alehouse, soon after.

Poe saw towering masts with creaking windlasses of a British East India ship with Chinese registry. On shore, he heard the racket of rolling barrels and wagon wheels. The crew was sawing and pounding in the shipyard, and nailing copper to the keel of a brig as it lie on the muddy bank of the bay after the tide had gone out that morning. One of the workmen was off-loading from the hold of the brig fireworks from a central compartment. Sailors were unloading cargo so it could be weighed on the customs service scales at the wharf: ebony, ginseng, rum, cloves, tea, molasses, pepper, ginger, ivory, Indian madras, Canton silks and casks of wine. In the shadows outside a Government bonded warehouse sat a thousand chests of Earl Grey tea. The U.S. Customs agent weighed each one on the customs scales. The tea merchant weighed each one on his tripod scales and off-loaded them into his counting house.

Poe entered, seeking informants, his eyes scrutinizing the faces he passed, and his fingers rubbing a cigar.

Poe showed the brightest man he saw an artist's drawing of Mary Rogers.

"Morning, what's your name?" Adam Wall said.

"Did you see this woman here before?" Poe asked him.

"Ha-ha, husky, hoarse-like," Adam Wall said.

"What do you do?" Poe asked.

"Carriage driver," Adam Wall said. Poe and Adam Wall looked out the window at his carriage standing waiting on the wharf.

A pirate sat next to Wall. He had one ear cut off and had a raven feather tucked into his kerchief as a symbol of a crime of passion.

"Come in at 4 bells," the pirate said. "Bonny."

"Swaying to the music," Adam Wall said.

The pirate laughed his coarse, bitter laugh.

"What did you see in her eyes?" Poe said. They did not respond. "Pale. Lifeless. Blank."

"The beast," Wall said. "Her guy."

"Bite your tongue," the pirate said.

"Who was she with?" Poe said.

"Who knows? Slippery bastard," the pirate said.

"And what about her? Exotic?" Poe asked.

"Like to run her through," the pirate said.

"What did he look like?" Poe said.

"Double-crosser," Adam Wall said.

"Were they taking drugs?" Poe said.

"I do not know nothing," Adam Wall said.

""Was the man providing her with opium?" Poe said. "Was she dreamy? We all have feelings which are forbidden."

"Marry your demons, man. It's an unholy life, anyway," the pirate said.

Poe looked down under the table then. He saw both of the

pirate's legs were cut off. Poe walked out then.

"Need a way?" Adam Wall said. But Poe kept walking.

Anderson had been staying in Manhattan, while the construction crew was building the cabin in New Jersey. But sometimes, like today, he came over to inspect the construction. The cabin was transforming into a three-story pseudo-mansion with a whitewashed false front. The architect and the workmen were happy the cabin was sprawling. Anderson's wealth and stability was theirs too while the project continued.

A white palisade overrun with English ivy shut off the property from a big thicket. The cabin, which was slowly being transformed into a mansion, was as wide as it could be, but it was only as deep as it had to be for the sake of appearance. The cabin was becoming a prinked out showpiece for the good life. This was just the big lie. Behind that was Anderson's mask.

Anderson was playing out every night and day for his audience of hoods and club-goers a forged desire for Mary Rogers. The opposite of guilt, is what Anderson wanted to exhibit, so he took the initiative. But he was lying through his teeth. He had no real desire for Mary Rogers. He was only jealous that anyone else should have her. His true desire was to spark Mary Rogers's passion and force it to smolder under his power.

Welch cranked the sailboat up the tracks into the boathouse for waxing. Welch was a bullet-headed workman who played his boss for all he was worth. Welch could handle the give and take in any job, but he had a long memory for what Anderson owed him. Fair is fair, Welch would say, but it was Welch who decided what was fair in the long run. Welch was just not as sociable as Anderson.

Anderson turned and growled down from the cabin toward the sinking sun. Anderson could hear along the shoreline the wild boys slinging insults at each other. When they would quit, the crickets would start clicking in their trilling tone. The cicadas would start their grating creak. The windmill would go on cranking. Anderson arched his neck to each side as if he were throwing a rope. His neck cracked and his backbone buckled for easement. He was wound too tight. Anderson's pit bull waddled out to greet him, with his smug pug. The pit bull looked up at the sky and sniffed and whimpered and reeled around and around. Anderson baited him to keep him quick and vicious. He pulled him up by the ears until he barked. Anderson himself seemed transformed, his snout flared out his stickery bristle of hair that stood up on his spine like a buzz-saw. His teeth were transformed into a grotesque under bite that could punch through skin like a belt-maker's awl.

Anderson bounded upstairs and banged back the door of the cabin porch. The porch was frowzy with magazines showing off heroes, and their continental style. Anderson saw something in Poe that was one of them, a military schoolboy who refused to snitch on his pals. A great impostor. Anderson stripped at the sink where Welch had gutted sunfish that morning.

Black beans had been simmering since last night. The sky was simmering, too, and now grew as purple as the skillet of beans. Tibbs was in the boathouse with Welch.

"I'm afraid mauve will be too "hot" for the upstairs doors," Welch said. "We could continue the yellow ochre on the doors and molding, though, to mute the brighter colors. By adding contrast, you see..."

Anderson howled downstairs at his whipping boy.

"Yes sir?" Welch said.

"I want a steam," Anderson said, "And a rub. Let us go down in the grotto until this storm blows over."

"Ten minutes, sir," Welch said. He then descended into the grotto underneath the cabin and disappeared into the plain stone structure to prepare the Russian steam bath. The grotto had once been just a cave. Anderson had constructed a cabin overhead. Welck slipped past a vault that held secret papers locked away. Welch stripped and put on a lightweight robe and some slippers. Welch's vague and befuddled appearance gave way to his quick uptake and thoroughness in kitchen prep-work and other small tasks. He slipped on the owl-like horn-rims he used for reading to check all the details. The liquor was stored in a separate room.

Then Anderson walked in, stripped for the steam. Welch popped up and showed Anderson into the sweat room with its rough stone oven, and dribbling spigots.

"Sit," Welch said. They sat on towels on one of three stone layers, and Welch worked as Anderson grunted and sprung his tensions and brayed like a bull in a chute. After ten minutes, when Anderson's ears were red and crisp, Welch poured a bucket of cold water on his head.

"Where is she?" Anderson started in.

"Anybody's guess, sir," Welch squeaked, and opened a bottle and poured Anderson a drink.

The pit bull pricked up his ears and walked to the boathouse to see who was coming. Welch went over too when he heard the sound of footsteps on the walkway. Anderson gargled a mouthful of liquor and spit it out. It sizzled when it hit the stones. "Where the Hell is she?" Anderson groaned. "I should have beached and gutted that boat and shredded the sails and whipped that girl with the bloody oar. How far away could she get in one hour?"

The Anderson imitated himself, "Are you sleeping with him?" Anderson chewed his lips and sucked the salt, fighting the steam. "I need a cure, boy. I got it bad. Kill her from my mind.

What kind of cure is there for me? I have got to work this poison out of my system. Dumb love hunt. What's it good for? Where is she?" Anderson took another bucket of water and poured it over his head and then he just sat and shook his head.

"I dreamed about her all night last night. I woke up and I felt like somebody had tried to strangle me in my sleep," Anderson said.

They heard the sound of someone opening the door upstairs, and the wail of the wind outdoors. Then Anderson had as much heat as he could bear. He stood up and walked over to the next room and then stepped down into the cool still dark green pool for a rinse. Then Anderson and Welch went into the rub-down room. The rub-down room in the grotto was stark from the bare torches, and had rocky walls, but the shadows were black-green and oily-looking. The sog danked every seam with oily resin. Welch rushed back and Anderson sank back in his version of relaxation.

"I have got a confession to make," Anderson said. "I like to follow through with young talent. I like to see somebody just starting out make it big. Never again will I let a young talent like Mary Rogers just slip by."

Then Welch started the rubdown.

"So what do you think it means? The dream I mean?" Anderson said. Welch mulled it over. I don't know how I'm going to make it."

Welch looked at Anderson and said, "Well, so, marry her."

Anderson rolled off the table and raised his arms over his head. He sprinted up the steps like a mad king.

"All I want is a little understanding!" Anderson roared. His tongue was dry, so he marched to the kitchen and drew some water. He looked out on the river and saw the storm pulling them into its floodgate shadow. "Where is she?"

Anderson appeared to be burning with passion and desire, but he raved from rage, and the rage began to spread.

"Where is she now?" Anderson said.

17 POE AND HER GHOST

MRS. CLEMM rose sleepily to catch Poe when he arrived at her boarding house on Carmine Street that night. She waved to the neighbors who shrank back from their windows. She closed the door behind him and then blocked his way.

"Where's the fire?" Mrs. Clemm said.

Poe was out of breath.

"I hope Sissy is sleeping easily," Poe said.

Sissy rasped hollowly. Then Poe exhaled wearily.

"Sissy may get better. But she will never get well," Poe said. Then he whispered. "Muddie, laudanum will ease her suffering."

"Don't you kindle my temper, Eddie," Mrs. Clemm said.

Poe checked his pocket-watch.

"Don't mind me," Mrs. Clemm said. She exited to the kitchen. She took out of the cupboard every ingredient she had to make a meager meal: left-over corn cakes and salt pork and kidney beans and a jar of tomatoes and a sack of flour and a crock of butter and one egg and a box of tea.

Poe entered the kitchen and picked at the morsels of food. He discovered the sugar bowl was empty and took one last taste by licking his finger. He discovered the saltbox was empty and took one last taste by licking his finger again.

"Get out of my kitchen," Mrs. Clemm said. She discovered the breadbox was only crumbs. She tried to press them back into shape but they fell like grains of sand. She sighed at the prospects. She took 4 clattering plates down from the cabinet and laid them out next to the fixings.

"You are inspired," Poe said.

Mrs. Clemm swatted at his fingers and then began cooking. She took the breadcrumbs and breaded the pork and fried it in the skillet.

"Get me those tomatoes. And the beans," Mrs. Clemm said. Poe plopped them into the pot.

Mrs. Clemm put the kettle of water on to boil and reused

the last tealeaves. Poe stoked the fire. Then Sissy entered the kitchen, sleepwalking.

Muddie began showering her with endearments.

"You look so pretty," Mrs. Clemm said. Then she asked Poe. "Doesn't she look sunshiny?"

Sissy was shy. She was paler and in the light from the window she had newly deepened lines on her face. She coughed. Poe moved Sissy to the piano bench and when Sissy was reluctant, he pulled Sissy close to him on the piano bench and began playing.

"What are you scheming?" Sissy asked Poe.

"I am finishing my story," Poe said. Poe leaped up then and playfully prowled the shadows of his house to entertain his wife, then stepped into the light with mischief in his eyes. Then Poe held up his notes for the Snowden's Ladies Home Companion story.

"Is this your story, finally?" Mrs. Clemm said. She was annoyed.

"The truth. So far. *The Mystery of Mary Rogers*. It will be the first of two parts," Poe said.

He took out a cigar wrapped in tin foil marked Anderson's Solace Tobacco, licking his smiling lips puckishly.

"More murder," Mrs. Clemm said.

Poe mirrored her scornful expression and shook his head.

"People believe that the girl was the victim of a gang of roughnecks. But I will indicate the assassin to revive investigation," Poe said.

"I'll read it when I find the time," Mrs. Clemm said.

"I'm glad... " Sissy said, stifling a cough, "You have friends here. But I miss Richmond."

Then Poe took Mrs. Clemm aside and began whispering in her ear.

"I want to free you from your alarm about our future fortune," Poe said.

Mrs. Clemm pretended to strangle Poe then, but he broke free.

"With kisses?" Mrs. Clemm said. "How much will they pay for your story?"

Poe's eyes were downcast. He takes his pen and scrawls over the zeroes and then transforms them into a caricature of a grotesque satanic figure. Poe covers his face with the page as a mask and points to the numbers.

"If my current boss doesn't value my contributions, I'll start a magazine of my own. I've met some possible backers. How do you like this: The Broadway Journal?" Poe said.

Mrs. Clemm mouthed the "zero," and grinned sardonically and turned away bitterly. As Poe stepped toward her, she pulled a bag of radishes from the floor and threw fistfuls at his masked face.

"Eddie!" Mrs. Clemm said. She threw her hands up in frustration and despair and turned away from him. She hatefully scraped butter on dry cornbread that crumbled away under the knife. She opened the cupboard door. The shelves were empty. "Radishes? But what about Sissy? She needs care." As Mrs. Clemm pulled from Poe's hands the mask he was holding, she read the frustrated meaningless figures and the grotesque caricatures and she threw the page in boiling water. The ink separated from the paper pages. The water became inky.

"Even if you do not recognize my talent, others do," Poe said.

"I pity you," Mrs. Clemm said. "You believe your talent places you above all the rest of us. But Sissy and I can't live on dreams. Thank God you have your job to fall back on."

Poe reacted to Muddie's anxiety with uneasiness. Poe heard something then, and he looked up at a silhouette of Sissy on the wall. Sissy sang in the next room Liszt's "Scenes From Childhood" but its tones were flowing slower and faltering. Poe listened more closely but all he heard now was the rustle of leaves brushing against the window.

"Eddie?" Poe could hear Sissy whispering.

Poe rushed into the front room. Sissy tried a reassuring, flustered smile.

"Let me be," Sissy said bitterly. "I am cold." Her

consciousness faded and her expressed morbid sadness. Poe

walked Sissy to her bed and kneeling under the low ceiling, he

covered her over.

"Eddie?" Poe's dying wife whispered. She was his 19-

year-old wife and cousin, and she looked up at him with expressive

and poignant and intelligent eyes. Poe stood over her now because

he knew she was going to die soon and he wanted to be there for

her when she died.

Poe ran through his mind the complexity of his situation.

His terror at the expense and loss of control eminent in his wife's

death was trudging him down into the rut of magazines again. You

whore! He told himself. Why mask my troubles behind a dead

pan when underneath skulks a grisly heart? Poe tried to shake his

moodiness.

"Eddie," Sissy said.

Poe looked out the window, his gaze tucked under the

eaves. Poe knew he had to finish his story. He knew he had to

escape to his spacious study a floor below them. Sissy lay

restlessly on the straw mattress with Poe's West Point greatcoat wrapped around her, and the cat hugged close to her body for warmth. She twisted as if descending into sleep. She wrenched against the unforgiving chill, her body agonizing, grinding and shivering against the bitterly cold within her. Poe walked up to his writing desk.

"I must deliver my bones on deadline," Poe said. He covered his ears, escaping. Sissy's coughing echoed like rustling leaves in his ears. Poe could see in his imagination a bust of his hero Byron, exploding in a foundry and hurling splinters of cast bronze outward, annihilating its form and leaving it unrecognizable. Once Poe was upstairs at his writing desk, he drank from a vial of laudanum. In his imagination the bronze melted down in a whirlpool, and he sank into the lightness and buoyancy of the opiate.

"Milk of paradise," Poe said to himself. He sank back in his hard wooden chair and re-lit the cigar and concealed his mysterious craving for something more in the smoke illuminated by candlelight. Poe saw in his imagination his reflection dissolving into mist. Poe lit a cigar then. As he fell asleep, leaning back, slumped in his chair, he began to dream.

Poe recognized her face in the smoke. The smoke streamed out. Poe fantasized that he and Mary Rogers were floating through the window in smoke and fog, back in time and place to Manhattan, last year.

Poe reached for her shadow slipping up under the eaves. The feline shadow darted up through the window. Poe twisted, agonizing, shivering against the unforgiving chill of what he sees. The shadow bolted away.

The lonely reflection of Mary Roger's ghost appeared in the window. Her image was glazed across the grain of the blown-glass windows like the knap of ice cast in a subtle, vinegary tint.

Poe blinked and brushed his weary eyes, making the candle flutter. He stirred and then he walked to the window. Poe was shuddering and irritated.

"Hush!" Poe said.

As the face of Mary Roger's ghost surfaced closer, it appeared mask-like and brushed into the glass in a fading, eerie gloss. The doorbell whistled and jingled in the wind. Mary Roger's ghost tapped on the window.

Poe caught a glimpse of his face in the window, congealing with hers.

"Eddie?" Mary Roger's ghost echoed hoarsely, rattling the window. "Eddie?"

Poe opened the window. Her glow was cast on his face. Poe took her hand, but his fingers were coated with a chalky glow.

"You are more radiant than ever. You crossed back over the threshold. Show me what happened," Poe said.

Poe stood at the window with Mary Rogers and passed his hands across her forehead, intending to soothe her but she was restless, discontent. He gazed into her eyes, intending to mesmerize her. Her eyes become tired. Her lids quivered. The grandfather clock downstairs rang the half-hour.

"We disappear and return to God to act out our parts in some other region of space," Poe said. Poe remembered Mary had been in life a 25 year-old, pretty and courteous sales-girl and cigar-shop assistant of low status that Poe had met when he was buying a

cigar. She had become in the few years Poe knew her, an urbane

and articulate (meaning sarcastic) New Yorker. She had attempted

to appear debonair and obliging, but she was always alert, with

glittering eyes that made sweeping, watchful glances. Behind the

scenes, she had a dancer's sensual, walk, especially when she

would catch her own glance in the mirror. Consequently she had

been known for handling stress smoothly, with a willowy and fox-

like grace. But now, of course, she was dead and her ghost was

both a fantasy and a morbid obsession for him.

Her image was glazed across the grain of the blown-glass

windows like the knap of ice cast in a subtle, vinegary tint. Poe

saw her reflection and he blinked and he found himself again

tortured by her memory. He tried to brush away her memory from

his weary eyes. Then Poe walked to the window, irritated, and he

whispered at Mary's image but when his wife stirred, he quietly

said, under his breath as if it were to himself so he wouldn't wake

her, "Wash far away, wash far away."

But when he closed his eyes, Mary's face appeared in his

mind's eye: her face surfaced, mask-like and brushed into the glass in a fading, eerie gloss.

Then the bell at the front door whistled in the wind, echoing its daylight toll, stinging his ears, jangling his concentration. Hush! Poe shuddered furiously, and masked his furious thoughts as if he were still at the office, worrying as he labored at his pinpoint drudgework like a human question mark. The echo of a jangled barb again. And again. The buzzing wasp in his unction kept on droning. Then a small fist started tapping at the window, that little club prying in so close. Poe uncramped his legs and unkinked himself and strode forcefully away and then back to the window and shooed her away as you might a wasp.

Then Poe, exhausted, tilted wearily against the near side of the wooden window frame, and caught a glimpse of his face in the mirror, stern but uncertain, with a cool surface that never masked his troubles. He saw a dreamy, flawed visionary who idolized beauty; flawed because he knew Mary's ghost was releasing something animalistic inside his spirit, something morbid and bizarre.

Then: Bang. Bang. Bang. Mary rattled the window.

"What?" Poe rumbled. He tried to brush the stinger away.

"Eddie?" She spoke with a distant echo. Suddenly with the sound of her voice everything changed. The voice called from the dark side of the moon. The startling undertow drew Poe back in a cavernous wave of intuition meaning: what was and what will be are in motion.

Poe opened the window wishing to jump into her and she appeared beside him, a vision unveiled from his fantasies. She was an image of rare beauty, simple and elegant, with the fluid spring of a cat reaching up to him, so hopefully, and he yearned to cast his body into her, and feel her giving in like a soft stone. But the glow in her face was eerie, lunar, Giorgioniesque.

"Hello?" Mary Rogers said. She needed reassurance, Poe recognized, as all of us need reassurances sometimes while maneuvering the dead zone of our desires. "Hello?" An eternity wormed away before Poe would answer.

"What?" Poe conceded, still rankled.

"Eddie," Mary Rogers said.

Poe turned to her and opened his arms to her. The wooden floor creaked. Her face glowed with that lunar cast. She did not respond but seemed absent-minded. Her hand was unvarnished by the conventional cast and aspect of skin, but instead was plain and chalky. She had been dressed in a robe which had been stitched together loosely in the back. Her neck and breasts, which had been rich butterscotch glazed with stark white, and which had offered a texture that was sweet and soft like kid gloves, her skin that had been flawless, was now gessoed and bony underneath. Poe looked at her face and then he could never look away. Her face was gaunt. Her nose was extremely thin and quite small, like a little sea-bird's beak from one angle, and from another it was prominent and shaped with courage and boldness and with her intelligent nostrils streamlined. But, of course, it was her eyes that were molded and sculpted with ideal, sorrowful and intense eyelids, and accented by relaxed eyebrows that ran high, straight and strong. And when she began to talk she seemed a little shy and unsure as if she and Poe were strangers, as though he'd never give her credence or listen to her but he knew her spirit had been broken along with her life. But Poe still believed in her, because their relationship was founded on her strong and friendly sense of humor that had brought them together inside a crowded cigar shop.

"You crossed back over the threshold," Poe said.

"I wanted to stir up a little trouble," she said. Her voice was hoarse. "I wasn't put on this earth for any other high and mighty reason. Like you were. I have my own struggle."

"Are you coming back to life?" Poe asked her.

"How can a body with no soul be transformed?" Mary Rogers asked him.

"You're such a perfect matrix," Poe struggled to communicate with Mary but each word unsettled more his muddled thoughts. There had never been a harmony between them and still, Poe felt, what was and what will be are racing toward us and racing away from us all the time. Poe paced away across the room. She seemed as insubstantial as a figure painted on a scrim in sepia, and his meeting with her this way felt tenuous and hurried. He was annoyed, and disturbed.

"You know? There was a storm on the Hudson River. There was a squall..." Poe struggled for the words.

"I couldn't for the life of me break free from that overshadowing bastard's..." Mary said. Poe knew she was talking about Anderson, the owner of the shop-owner. He was, after all, the reason they had met. "He promised to deliver me..."

"But you died before it came about," Poe said. "And so, you're still a vision, and maybe you're still a fantasy for me, but I wish you weren't an illusion. I wish it had worked out between us." Poe realized when he heard myself give in that he was being seduced. Does she want me to sleep in her grave with her? He wondered.

"Distance lends enchantment," Poe said, struggling to maintain his sanity and his life. One contemplates a face and then, suddenly, notices its likeness to another. The face has not changed, and yet Poe felt differently about it.

"For me, your voice recalls another person's voice," Poe

tried to explain. But Poe didn't want to bring his dying wife into this. Poe tried to concentrate on his previous image of her face to keep her straight. He struggled because coming face to face with Mary Roger's ghost was no simple reaction, but a mixing of memory and sensation which seized and shaped her being with her previous duality of a transposed public and reclusive, secret self. Poe now felt himself building more into this shadow-person because he had been freed of his previous perception. Poe felt his ears ringing and he reeled in a quandary, as if his attention were divided by not-quite-simultaneous strikes of tonic and subdominant chords on a piano. It is the differences that make us aware of people's qualities at all. When we see similarities between one another, we become weak, as if our own motives are hidden from us. It may be that the reason given to others, and to us, for the explanations of our interests are invented after the inherently ambivalent fact, and composed to cover up a blind impulse, as the curtain to eclipse some necessarily fine and private place.

"There is no unselfish reason for me to become entangled

with you," Poe said.

"Any reason which speaks its name is suspect?" Mary said.

"I see you frozen in an eternal present tense," Poe said.

"Wedged between was and will be," Mary said, and her words rang as if she could read his mind.

"Won't you ever be in the past?" Poe said. "I can never find a way to accommodate you to my way of seeing the world."

"Your world has changed," Mary said.

Poe saw a shadow world opposite to the real world. The night: a shadow world, a negative world away from the light. Poe saw Mary Rogers like a negative that couldn't make sense, and couldn't be held up to scrutiny against the light. Only the outline of her shadowy figure took shape, and was sharpened against the deep background. In the negative world her figure walked like a ghost, blurring into the air around us. Her skull stood out, made of fog, the hollows of her eyes sucked in, sculpted more to express the yearning and need for life than eyes could. And Poe made his footsteps land on the dark floor, planting my feet one after another there, in between the furniture and the lights that turned themselves inside-out. But there she hovered. Anywhere out of this world. A body between places. Mary Rogers' were a pair of fascinated eyes that gazed into the dark sea of night at the bottom of the world. Mary Rogers walked made of light, the same light she walked through. She moved like a sculpted and artificial cloud interweaving in crossing currents. She dissolved into herself and then reappeared. Behind her reflections rippled on the glass and the glass breathed her in and breathed her out with the passing pressure of a puff of smoke. The illusions multiplied as curtains opened, and as layers of aimless air flowed away. Magic world that walks around us pulling birds from the air and dissolving blind men in the trees. Mary Rogers seemed to drift away, to wash far away, and Poe could not find a place for himself to light in his own home.

Then Mary Rogers's ghost hovered away into fog, her reflection rippling through the glass, dissolving and disappearing.

"Before I had you, I lived among strangers with not one soul to love me," Poe said. He walked to the window and saw her form joining the fog, dissolving into the trees and water. He sat, shaken.

18 THRUST OUT OF THE CHARMED CIRCLE

WHEN POE walked to John Anderson's Segar Store, he looked in from the street, seeing through the window, the cigar girl who was offering Anderson's Solace Tobacco wrapped in tin foil. Poe's face paled, his lips mouthed the name: Mary Rogers. He stormed through the front door.

The cigar girl, then turned away, unaware of Poe's entry and latched some cigars in a heavy humidor.

Poe stormed in and seized the shoulder of the cigar girl behind the counter, forcing her to drop the humidor, spilling the contents.

"Was this some twisted hoax?" Poe raged.

The cigar girl crumbled defensively and raised her hand to shield her face. Poe pulled her hand away and only then realized she was not Mary Rogers.

"Ask my boss," the new cigar girl stammered.

"Is he here?" Poe said.

"No, he's having a party tonight," the cigar girl said.

"I have been thrust out of the charmed circle of life," Poe muttered. Then he made his way uptown through Theater Alley.

The immigrants who hovered there in the squalid alleys and gutters to escape the heat and the night watch were talking.

"We thought the streets were paved with gold," one of the immigrants said to Poe. "They weren't even paved. We paved them. Now we sleep in them."

Poe imagined the Narrator of his tale had guided his mind to wander *en route*, and he dreamed up storm clouds transforming into an unknown beauty's face above the river, and he, himself, below, on solid soil.

Poe walked into The Falstaff Hotel on Sixth Street above Chestnut in Philadelphia, where actors and writers were meeting at about 8 A.M.

"I have understood some transcendentalism as a protest against spirituality and the doctrines of the Unitarians," Poe said.

The artist he was speaking to was a shadowy little man.

Paint stained his tiny hands. He moved Poe into a chair as if for his portrait. The artist harnessed Poe by the neck with his hand, and murmured something about Poe's *dénouement*, then scurried away. Poe watched the man's little feet fidgeting in the corner. Another actor perched like a black beast, gazing at him, secretively.

"Grotesque is some writers avidity to steal my work, like a mirror with a memory," Poe said.

"Sh-h," the artist said. "Do not move."

As the natural light descended through the window overhead, illuminating Poe, his disheveled brown hair seemed darker over his pale, high, pronounced forehead. Poe tried to study his reflection in the nearest window, nervously fussed with his hair, but gave up.

The artist walked to the candle-lit bar to develop his next riposte for Poe.

"You are a poet," the artist said. "Recite something for me."

"Some have a double life," Poe began playfully. "Which

springs from matter..." Poe's words came more forcefully, quickly and passionately. The artist poured something into a bowl supported above a spirit lamp, which he then lit (while avoiding inhaling the fumes). The artist gazed into Poe's eyes to judge his reaction and then he gazed back at him sharply.

Poe balanced a glass in his hands. Now, in the mirror, he saw a negative, shadowy image of himself, perhaps he saw himself half-positively and half-negatively. Poe tried to recognize himself in the likeness of his reflection in the window, but then he found his mind wandering to the pealing bells that echoed outside. He wondered what part of his spirit was echoed here. Then Poe shook his hand and resumed his recital.

"Matter and light, Poe said.

Poe looked at his frozen reflection and then, glancing at the mirror on the wall, he felt his own face moving self-consciously. He could hear out on the street a troupe of gypsies passing. A gypsy girl laughed and her jewelry jingled to the Haydnesque strands of a rondo, then faded.

"Solid and shade," Poe continued reciting. The shadow

soared overhead and then disappeared. His piercing gray eyes electrified Poe's sharp features during his quickly alternating moods. The shadow re-emerged as it winged through shafts of light, which descended into the dim bar. The artist listened nervously to Poe, witnessing what seemed like a wild flight of fancy.

"There is a two-fold Silence," Poe said. The ferry's horns echoed, fading, as Poe's face flickered in the light. The daguerreotype artist focused the image.

"Sea and shore," Poe said, looking up at the window and watching the sun glowing through a spider's wet web. Poe felt his collar scrape his neck and with his thin hands gesturing cockily, he hid the worn and frayed folds of his clean linen shirt, and then dropped his arms because his suit was shining at the elbow.

"Body and soul," Poe said to himself. A cloud swept overhead then, and the room grew dark as the shadows crossed over his face.

"One dwells in lonely places, his name's "No More," Poe said.

Then the artist smiled diplomatically and watched as Poe exited the gallery, his silhouette storming out into the misty, glowing cloud of vapor. Poe sliced through the evaporating mist, his face breaking through beams of sunlight. His shoes busked the grimy gridiron streets. Voices shouted and riggings clanged from wagons bound back from the market.

19 POE AT ANDERSON'S MANSION

AT ANDERSON'S mansion, at sundown, he unwrapped a ball of opium, revealing the reddish-brown cake. He lifted the opium to his nose and smelled deeply its intoxicating fragrance. He took a tiny pinch and tasted its bitterness. He rolled a ball the size of his little fingernail into a treacly pellet and lit his opium lamp. He hovered over its tiny, glowing flame, his eyes becoming suddenly frail and then his opium-shattered eyes lost their spark. He exited to rejoin the party he was hosting. Music by Chopin was playing.

Poe saw Anderson's mansion for the first time. It was the palace of a millionaire, with a private library, a court of palms and a banqueting hall. Poe saw that Anderson was formally dressed for a lavish dinner in tuxedo, holding a cigar, and stood with a laurel wreath perched on his head.

Poe sidled in through the side door and once inside, he overheard Anderson and a shipping magnate laughing together.

"Newsboys," Anderson said.

"Raw and vulgar and common," the shipper responded.

"These cynical critics climb out of their cellars to prance around with death," Anderson said.

"They terrorize the civilized," the shipper said.

"Playing every angle," Anderson said.

"That is true," the shipper said.

"Or untrue," Anderson said.

Then Anderson was shocked to see Poe, who had arrived uninvited, and he swept Poe aside.

"Imagine my surprise," Anderson said, coldly and distantly to Poe.

"I stopped into your smoke shop and I thought I saw Mary Rogers," Poe laughed.

"She's history," Anderson said. "Relax, why are you always suspicious?"

"Can we speak in private?" Poe said.

"Have you come to confess?" Anderson smiled.

Anderson led Poe through the crowded room where a

masked ball was going on. A horse ran on a treadmill before a revolving backdrop, the stage was still set for a performance of Racine's Phaedre. Props cluttered the backstage area: an elephant head, an Aladdin's cave, lions, and gargoyles.

"Mr. Poe, I'd like to introduce..." Anderson started to say amid the throng.

Poe reached out to shake a woman's hand, but the passing crowd pulled their hands apart and she was swept away. Anderson and Poe continued through the masked crowd.

"Prominent theater people and politicos?" Poe asked.

"Whigs from up at that log cabin Tippecanoe Club, where they still initiate voters with hard cider, drinking bumpers for spiritual improvement," Anderson said.

"There is truth in wine honest men blush to utter," Poe said.

"You've been known to backslide from temperance," Anderson said.

"The bar is more down to earth than where I've been reading my poetry, at parties for the well-to-do," Poe said.

"Society is a new, powerful force," Anderson said.

"My study escaped society before, Poe said, remembering. "I thought you explored your soul in nature, your predatory nature."

"I like a new religion. For a new industrial world," Anderson said.

Anderson and Poe stepped into the office and Anderson closed the door.

"I want you to come with me," Poe said.

"Where are we going?" Anderson asked.

"Over near Elysian Fields," Poe said. He saw that Anderson seemed nervous. "Why are you looking so skittish?"

"I feel like a prisoner in an invisible cell," Anderson said.

"Just retrace Mary Rogers's steps with me," Poe said.

"She disorganized everything," Anderson said.

Anderson felt Poe questioning Anderson's intentions, so Anderson became more hidden and defensive and high-strung.

"Were you using Mary Rogers as a spy?" Poe asked.

"Don't play games with me," Anderson said.

"Do you think she crossed over to the other side?" Poe asked.

"You've got more wild-eyed notions than a schoolboy," Anderson said. Then Anderson swept Poe outside, leaving the party behind through a rear entrance. Poe steeled his reserve. "She has got me run aground and working double tides now. What are you thinking?"

"You knew that Spencer's uncle is a judge and he was planning to run for mayor," Poe said.

"Liar! You're a demon," Anderson said, seizing Poe by the collar.

20 LOSS IS DEAD

POE HAILED an omnibus and rode south to the Northern Hotel by the Cortland Street Ferry. When he got out, he read the sign: Port of New York, The next steamship to arrive: from Liverpool, the Acadia, from Boston, the Caledonia.

Poe boarded the Hoboken ferry and rode into Bay, which opening to the south toward Staten Island. He was sprayed by the chop, gray-green and rough. The red beacon bobbed. He felt the boom and the chug and the drum of the grinding mechanical engine as the boat slapped against the slow, dark roiling water. As he looked down into the surface of the water and he imagined his face mirrored. He cradled his aching skull. His image in the water shattered into fragments and reeled away in a whirlpool and when he looked up he was gazing into mist.

Looking back toward Manhattan, he remembered Revelations 17:1: And upon her forehead was a name written: Mystery.

Four bells rang from the bridge as they arrived in Hoboken.

Poe exited the ferry and walked the three miles north, through Elysian Fields, and crossed Ludlow's Farm.

Poe approached Nick Moore's Roadhouse near Weehawken, and as he came near the shore, a noisy fight erupted in the crowd of butcher-boys on the mud bank.

Mrs. Frederica Kellenback Loss was the keeper of the roadhouse, whom everyone called Freddy. She was intelligent, good-looking, age 30, with a thick German accent, and she welcomed everyone with familiarity.

"Pay no attention to those butcher-boys down at that rum-hole on the mud bank," Freddy Loss said to Poe as she served him a beer.

"I am following the trail Mary Rogers left behind. Did you see her?" Poe asked.

"Oscar!" Freddy called out.

Oscar appeared in the doorway. He was her argumentative 15-year-old son, a bitter, lying juvenile delinquent. He came in from the stable, reining in a mare.

"What do you want?" Oscar said.

"What about Mary Rogers?"

"Bolted off her high horse," Oscar said.

"You're a rutting boar like your father, God have mercy on him," Freddy said with disgust. Poe was sitting back an observing the layout of the location. "If Mary Rogers was at our tavern..." Freddy said, conspiratorially sharing beers from a pitcher. "Right where you're sitting," she said secretively.

"Sure," Poe said.

"On that hot Sunday last," Freddy said. "She might have straggled in with the ferry crowd to escape the heat."

"All hot and bothered was she?" Poe said.

"Probably with a companion," Poe said.

"What time was it?" Poe asked.

"3 P.M.," Freddy said.

"Sure," Poe said.

"The kitchen was open," Freddy said.

"She staggered in all alone with her face hacked up," Poe said.

"She came in with a dark young man," Freddy said. "Swarthy. She must have been sociable and outgoing."

"Easy?" Poe said.

"Modest," Freddy said.

"Strolling the docks?" Poe said.

"She was dressed in a light, peculiar striped dress," Freddy said. "She came in to get out of the rain. "I'll have a lemonade, she said to me."

"Specialty of the house," Poe said.

"Then, when the rain stopped falling, she and the swarthy man, they left then. She smiled and bowed prettily at the door," Freddy said.

"Which way did they go? Straight to Hell in a hand basket?" Poe said.

"Into the woods," Freddy said. "Then a gang of roughnecks came in. Every Sunday, crowds of roughnecks, armed with sticks, arrive in boats and go to a rum house in a shanty on the mud bank and drink."

"Then why did they come in here?" Poe said.

"To get out of the downpour," Freddy said. "They roared into the kitchen and ate cake and near dark, they walked out without paying, and stormed off toward Weehawken Hill, following the route Mary Rogers had also taken."

"What did you do? Put it on their account?" Poe said.

"I mind my own business," Freddy said. "Near dark I told Oscar to drive a bull down the lower road to Ludlow's farm. "A few minutes later I heard choking and a moan: 'Oh, oh, God.' I heard the screams and Ossian, heard them also down in the cellar. He walked up and said, 'what's wrong, mama?' I said, "I fear the bull has tossed Oscar." I ran over to Ludlow's farm and found Oscar. I said, 'you are safe here. You come home with me now.'
"

"You'd lie and she'd swear to it," Poe said to Oscar and Freddy.

"You are going to miss your deadline, newsboy," Freddy said.

"Show me," Poe said.

Poe and Freddy Loss walked over to the thicket south of Nick Moore's Roadhouse and Freddy led Poe into the woods.

"My boys were collecting sassafras bark," Freddy said. Poe and Freddy Loss then penetrated a small thicket. Poe held up the briars for Freddy to pass under and they struggled up the side of the hill. They walked along a path. They came upon 4 very large stones, forming a kind of seat, with a back and footstool to it. The boughs and briar bushes are twined thickly around it. On the upper stone lay a white garment.

"Somebody left their shirt," Freddy said.

"Razor sharp," Poe muttered.

"It is a woman's petticoat that has been darned in a hurry," Freddy said.

"You know your needle-work," Poe said. "Over here. A second stone with a woman's identical silk scarf."

"It is all crumpled up, as if were torn off," Freddy said, eyeing Poe's acceptance. "Forcibly. Look! In this little hollow."

Poe found a parasol, jammed between the chair-like stone and the trunk of a small tree. He picked up a pair of gloves.

"Turned inside out," Poe said. "As if they had been forcibly drawn from her hands in a hurry. What's this?" Poe picked up a pocket-handkerchief. He turned it over in his hand. It was marked M.R. "Mary Rogers." Poe walked on, his eyes gazing down at the ground. As he fiddled with the handkerchief, he eyed Freddy Loss suspiciously. "Is this what Mary Rogers was wearing at your tavern?"

"Evidently yes," Freddy Loss said.

"Evidently," Poe said. "Torn out as she was dragged through. One piece of the dress was so doubled as to have a thorn three times through it. The place around was stamped about, and the branches were broken and roots bruised and mashed as if the scene of a very violent struggle. The marks of high-heeled boots were very plain. It appears that the girl was placed upon the middle broad stone, her head held forcibly back, and then and there

235

she was horribly violated by several rowdies and ultimately strangled. Because at a spot not far from the river, two rails were taken down as if both had been carried from the scene. I've got enough for the first part of my story. The extraordinary features in a mystery do not hinder a solution, but instead make it more certain. I use an unorthodox and daring approach. I discard the interior and examine the minute details."

"Who killed this girl?" Freddy asked. Oscar and Freddy stood closer together. Their expressions were agitated. Poe looked them over and judged them.

Freddy and Oscar then backed into the corner anxiously and whispered.

"Poe has such a high-handed, self-confident..." Freddy whispered.

"It's like a gallows, you know?" Oscar said. "The way he cuts the wood and drive in the nails and Bang! The trap-door swings."

"Stop it!" Freddy whispered to Oscar. "He's accusing us of

murder."

Oscar drew a Colt from his belt.

You're not turning me in," Oscar said. "I'm not going to hang for this."

"Neider das Geschütz," Freddy said. Oscar fired the Colt. Freddy caved in her gut. Oscar stood over his mother. Blood surged onto her blouse, She paled and lost strength. Freddy Loss tried to stand but her legs buckled and she fell into Oscar's arms. He carried Freddy Loss's body upstairs. Poe could see she was about to die.

"Gespenst!" Freddy was raving incoherently.

Oscar Loss sat in a chair in the corner, crying, and "Talk to me."

Justice Gilbert Merritt entered the bedroom then and walked up to Freddy Loss's bedside.

"I was downstairs," Justice Merritt said. Then he heard Mrs. Loss. "What is she ranting about?" he said to Poe. "Nonsense." Then he spoke to Oscar. "She is calling for you."

Oscar Loss hugged his mother and she stopped.

"She is dead," Oscar said.

"You close up the tavern now," Justice Merritt said to Oscar. And he brought him in to jail.

21 POE EARNS HIS BREAKFAST

POE WOKE before dawn and walked down to the Herald to find Tibbs.

"Let us go out fishing," Poe said.

"Is it already daylight in the swamp?" Tibbs said.

"Let's go earn our breakfast," Poe bellowed and he rousted Tibbs out of the cocoon-like office. They crossed the island to the North River. And took the ferry to Hoboken.

"We will rent a dinghy and two poles and a stash of minnows, alive, and a handful of worms," Poe said to the boatman there.

"My stomach is growling already," Tibbs said. They rowed out a hundred yards.

"Have you ever heard of noodling?" Poe asked Tibbs.

"Doodling?" Tibbs said. "Sure."

"Noodling," Poe corrected him. "You reach in underwater, under a rock for a fish."

"Are you crazy?" Tibbs said.

"I heard about a man who reached in noodling with a gaffer's hook and they found the hook next spring in the jaw of a hundred-pound fish," Poe said. "But they never found the noodler."

Then Poe rowed them to a stand of partially submerged logs. Tibbs got a strike near the roots of an elm on shore, and began wrestling in a five-pound bluefish. Tibbs reeled him in. When they returned to the dock, the boatman started cleaning the fish with a Norwegian filet knife. Then he fed the guts to an alley cat and then horse flies started appearing. The boatman wrapped the fish in butcher paper.

"What do people do on this river-bank?" Poe said.

"They swim in the shallows," the boatman said. "Some slip into the woods, before the hills start to climb."

Poe nodded his thanks and he and Tibbs walked north toward Nick Moore's Tavern.

The woods were never still. The river was stunning with its

earthly force flowing forever south. Poe found a place where brush had been dragged, but no useful evidence. Venus rose in the west and cast an unearthly glow.

"That star has no fire," Poe said. Then he began musing about Mary Rogers. "Mary Rogers slipped out of the water, her body glowing against the woods, as if she were a luminous blue shadow rubbed out of the deeper black night and the gray shadows around her. She did not put her clothes back on, but she sat down on them in the warm, still air. Her killer slipped out of the water too, and he started building a bon-fire.

"Oh, yeah?" Tibbs said. Poe looked up at the stars pinned against the gathering indigo.

"There is no end to how deep the deepest black can get, is there?" Poe said. "To think our sun is a star. Polaris," Poe pointed. "The North Star."

Tibbs tossed a handful of stones, listening for the brushing sweep as they hit.

"Mary Rogers huddled close to her killer," Poe said.

"Could you take care of me? She said. I believe everything you say, her eyes told him." She stared down at her knees that she had pulled up against her chest. Then she looks up and smiled at him. "This is the perfect place for us, she was thinking. Secluded." They were in the shadows, under a tree.

"He was a hunter, and she enchanted him," Poe said. "Her desire was real. But she was skittish, leery of all men. But she could not sense the dark side of his nature. She could not become the force for her own deliverance. Because her clothes were a little wet."

"Let us go have a look," Poe barked to Tibbs. "Another dark day in a dark year."

"Her dead body must have been pulled to the shore, sir," Tibbs shouted back toward Poe. Tibbs was trying to draw a bead on the horizon. Poe found a dory and Tibbs climbed in. Then Poe bulldogged the oar around toward his pier. Clouds killed the light and then cleared. Poe's face was grimacing stiff in the breeze, eyes squinting. His focus was cloudy. Poe grunted. His words were lost in the roar of the squall. Poe strong-armed his oars, plowing deep furrows in the river's green surface.

"This is no good, sir," Tibbs said. He looked back over Poe's head. "There's something bad in the air."

Poe was dizzy. The world seemed dizzy. The air ahead was still and thick and strange. Poe tried to clear his head, but he was sluggish. The sky behind them was jammed up with dark blue and brown and yellow-green balconies of clouds.

"Nice quiet paradise?" Poe growled. His cunning never let him rest. He craned around and bucked his nose up toward the southwest. Clouds inked over the sun. A distant pillar of thunderstorms swooped down slowly, reeling toward the river like tea down a jammed up drain. Tibbs's burly hands balanced against the reeling dory. The water chopped. The dory bucked.

"I thought this was going to clear," Tibbs said.

"It did not clear," Poe said. "Thunder showers." Poe sighted the cloudbanks and winced. "I like a good storm. Washes the air," Poe barked.

"Don't you think we should head back, sir?" Tibbs said.

"The Night Watch will nail her killer in good time. You can count on that. The waves are coming on pretty high."

"It's just a little chop," Poe steadied his path. "You're rust-proof aren't you?" The bay and the river rushed together now, so that the water was cut in roiling zigzags. "Get me the spyglass." Poe's contempt foamed through his teeth. Poe brought the ferry landing into focus. He scanned the fishing boats and their nets and lines.

"Those two boys who found Mary Rogers's body, they were probably fishing and she fouled their lines," Poe said.

Poe racked the oars and kneeling, stripped his clothes. Then Poe coiled to spring. He came up fighting the chop. He spit out the water he had sucked in. He was treading water until he turned onto his back. He struggled against the current and growled. He was winded. Poe rubbed his face with his palms. A current was sweeping cold, deep down, but the water on the surface was pulling Poe away. He was struggling. Then he told himself to calm down, get the feel for it, quit fighting it. Poe paddled on his side like a crab because the wind had picked up and the chop was high. When Poe was winded, he gave in for a minute and let the water carry him back. Poe swam alongside the dory and lurched the inboard by hanging in the water before he could throw his leg up and pitch himself inside.

"You got back," Poe said.

Poe heard Tibbs retching.

"Do it back there," Poe said. Then Tibbs was sick. But he crawled back and did it out of the way. Then he got water and washed off his face and sat up straight and stiff and watched the horizon. Then he was cold, so he put on his jacket and watched the horizon. Poe ground his jaw, sucking the bitterness through his back teeth.

Poe moored the dory. Poe lunged up onto the dock and spun away from the gathering storm and stomped up the slope toward the cabin. The windmill halfway up from the dock had been creaking slowly in the scant wind all day, with its skeletal vigilance. Now the pinwheel spun into the northeast and picked up speed.

"This is how it might have worked," Poe said to Tibbs.

"The dark man was trusted by Mary Rogers. They met in Manhattan and he brought her over to this resort. Then, when the rain started, they ducked into Nick Moore's Tavern. The dark man was watching over Mary Rogers, but with an evil intent. Mary Rogers lay unsuspecting, with her eyes closed to the world. She felt a shadow pass over her like a suspicion.

" 'Did you miss me?' Mary Rogers whispered in his ear. 'Let us get married'. Then the dark man made angry accusations. He was strict; maybe he did everything by the letter of the law. She was smoky, more vaporous and dreamy. She was trembling with unholy dread at his fury, so she would smother her fear in his shoulder and be anesthetized by his scent, maybe even laying her head on his lap. Then the last thing she would say would be: wake me up after my nap. He was silent, with her under his spell. Not really a spell. A trance. Then when she woke up, perhaps she danced around the argument at first. But eventually the arguing started.

"Then the dark man started cutting. He strangled her, and then he cut a spiral along her eye-brows and her lips and along the

246

shape of the bones in her face, along this wedge here by her eyes."
Mary Rogers's murder had been badgering Poe's conscience as if
she were his own flesh and blood. His own little girl growing up
too fast. Mary Rogers, you are sharper than a serpent's tooth, Poe
imagined. Sometimes the words to make things right just would
not fit together. He would think of something, and then it would
come out to high and mighty. Thankless child. He could not think
of how to say it. So he burrowed inside his imagination and tried
to match those images with proof.

" 'Mary Rogers, you are running wild. You cannot be
chasing around with card-readers. You cannot be seeing someone
else, some prodigal son'," Poe said, riding on his flight of
inventiveness. "He was not the marrying kind, who wanted to
settle down with her. Perhaps he was already married. Maybe he
was weary of the deception he had to keep up with his own wife.
She was probably after him like a chigger at home.

"He was probably scraped by the hedge, these stickers
could have whipped his face and arm as he brushed them away,"
Poe showed Tibbs. "It was only an acre, here, where the struggle

occurred. Hacking her down like a jonquil.

"But then he had to bind her up and drag her to the river," Poe said. "The quivering must have stopped by then. The clouds were starting to clear by then as if she could have climbed up to heaven on them, across the blue forever. The sounds of people returning to Manhattan were clear from the ferry. But the dark man pulling her body was flattening the woodchuck holes around the elms, around the Indian gum and sassafras. He was sweating, starting to learn to live with his guilt. He probably denied the reality of what he had just done. The whole world seemed to be going away and he had to take care of this business. He had trapped himself inside this diminishing spiral forever.

"If I could read his mind, if I could look down from up above through the eyes of God, along this soggy stretch here, with the dark man scraping the mulch off of his boots. Some of may have dried already, so he peeled that off in starchy sheets and chucked it into the brush or the creek. The frogs hated when he tossed something in there, like that. They eased into their little holes in the riverbed like they just got the idea to get some sleep.

The dark man was sweating and the air was muggy and hard to breathe. But he had to keep going to the river with her body. The echo of her pleading was ringing in his ears. Did he think he was going to live forever? I have got all the time in the world. But then he would have to keep that memory inside. His mind would wander, and then making circular clockwork patterns with smaller and smaller trails like a maze he was shutting himself into.

"That night, after the searing, blistering high noon, and the rain, then it smelled fresh, so she must have fallen asleep in a dry spot as if she were planted," Poe said. "The dark man must have lurched along the knoll, the sound of people drumming and thundering beyond the trees.

"There she was, the vessel created so that the hole, the cavity, the space created by the form was the important part, and now she lay shattered," Poe said. Maybe they were having a baptism near here, singing "On Jordan's Stormy Banks." A flood of sunlight washed across the river and rushed on. Then the sun ducked behind a cloud.

Poe meditated for a while. You cannot expect signs. It is a

wonder anybody would think you could.

Off in the distance, they saw the purple where some thunderheads were coming up, and going to rain. But they just kept going. At first it was just a sprinkle. Then the rain started coming down pretty good in torrents, in drops about the size of peas, blobby and full of air. The rain was like a thresher cutting them apart. They had to get out of it and right now. They ducked into Nick Moore's tavern. But they wanted to be alone. They walked out the back, perhaps by the barn, where the help was working, maybe they saw something."

Poe started humming a hymn and the tranquilizing sweetness and the familiar old white gospel flow of the melody and the clockwork assurance it gave him that something would live on after he was gone to a better place. The Poe sunk into one of his moods as he tried to pull away the hazy curtain of the past and see through the riddle clearly.

Tibbs saw a sardonic, paradoxical character, a madman and renegade, with a melancholy disposition.

Poe was driving himself through a baptism of fire. He was

letting his words drip tortuously now, drop by fleck. He sipped a cigar and waved away the smoke, spitting, pinching his eyes with finality, and sweeping a dismissing hand toward Tibbs.

"You must focus, see the details clearly," Poe said. Poe exhaled, his purple tongue seared, eyes stinging. Smoke rose from his sagging face, hanging epicene and blunt. He squinted his cold-toned eyes because of the choking fumes. Poe put his cold, chalky fingers down into the gouges along the murderer's path and stirred up a little dust.

"When I think of Mary Rogers, left barren by that snake, and the solitary incompleteness of murder," Poe said. "We know who we are, we do not know what we will become. Lately my dreams have been like this: It is dark and I am prowling around this place. It is very late and everyone is asleep. I am the only one awake in the world. The dark is so dark, that it looks smoky; it has an atmospheric quality, a grainy quality. I want to get to the other side of the river, but I cannot get through. This is the source of my regret."

When Poe returned home with the fish wrapped in butcher

paper, he handed the package to Muddie.

"What is this? Are you hungry?" Muddie asked him. She unwrapped the fish and turned it over and sniffed it and suddenly recoiled. "You should have salted this."

"What for?" Poe asked.

"Salt keeps things fresh," Muddie said.

"Can you add more salt and make it fresh?" Poe asked her. "Can you save it?" Muddie pulled out a container of rock salt from the cupboard, removed the lid and poured it over the fish, sprinkling salt over his boots in the process. Then she slipped away toward her bedroom in frustration. She lunges up the stairs, its oak steps groaning. Poe could hear her crying. The fish stared up at Poe in ruin. Muddie's door slammed above and the walls and stairs resonated with finality.

"There is no need to get morbid about it," Poe shouted at the door. Then he brushes up in a pan the fish and salt and let it sink into the trash. Then he sat at the counter. He was groggy. Darkness gathered inside. Then Poe whistled as he brooded over how he could have married into this family. When he walked upstairs, he discovered Sissy was pretending to be asleep. Poe walked into his study and wrote until he awoke with a jolt in the middle of the night. His body felt tough from rowing. He could not settle himself into a deep sleep in his chair, but he was lost in a puzzling maze of dreams. In his dream, Poe was feverishly chasing Mary Rogers up some stairs. Hundreds of people were watching but Poe had no connection to any of them. Water began pouring down the stairs and Poe fought his way up.

"I do not like Sissy's bed where it is," Muddie said to Poe when they met in the hallway. "Move it."

"But she feels the morning sunlight here," Poe said.

"Move it," Muddie said. "Or I will hire somebody to do it for me. What do you want for breakfast?" Poe saw she had dressed herself up in a more attractive dress with heavy lipstick and eye make-up.

22 SHE IS IN HIS DREAMS

POE STANDS rocking on the crosstree. The mast sways, the boom swings, each plank groans as he struggles to secure the jib. Gravity's invisible force drives him toward the ground. He knows if he gives in and jumps then he will go down. Dying will take care of all his problems, resolve his fear. But he will not quit. The hull sways, the threat of collapse is all that stands. If he falls down to the bay, then gravity's transforming power will let him rest. His vertigo keeps him undead, fearful, unsafe, teetering, the telltale fluttering in his face.

Then Poe felt himself falling into Mary Rogers in his dream.

"I will wash your back," Poe offered to Mary Rogers.

"I will do it myself," Mary Rogers said. "I am in a hurry."

"Where are you going?" Poe asked Mary Rogers. She looked away mysteriously.

"I am losing faith in our future," Mary Rogers said.

Poe could not function in isolation, interpreting the cryptic letters, face-to face with his double, the mirror image reflected in the windows foreshadowed too much.

Mary Rogers lay in the bathwater, rocking the water back and forth and then sprinkling in eucalyptus salts. Poe sat down on the edge of the water. Mary Rogers's body floated, bobbing up and down in the water. Poe put his hand on the back of her neck and ladled water over her hair.

"There is no reason to be afraid," Poe said. Mary Rogers lets herself float back against his arm. "I have got you." She was light and buoyant resting in the cradle of his arm. Her hair and her face were wet.

"One time I brought home a stray cat that reminds me of you," Poe started telling Mary Rogers. "I made a place for it in the corner with a crate and a feather pillow. But the very next night the cat ran away. The strayness was in here nature, through and through."

"I stray," Mary Rogers said. "I never know where that might take me." Then she took a wet navy-blue washcloth and slapped it over her face and she lolled around in the bath and slid

under the suds. She had let a cigarette made of tobacco blended

with clove. She picked the cigarette up from the soap dish and

inhaled and then blew the smoke and then waved the smoke away

from her face and gazed at the filigreed form absent-mindedly.

Mary Rogers swept the water easily over her breasts. She looked

up with her wet hair slicked back.

"I believe people, everyday people, can be gifted with the

gift of prophecy. That is how they see signs. When I was twelve I

had been having a crying spell and I saw an angel. He was my

guardian angel, standing under the gas light at the corner. It was

dark-haired but it did not have any sex. I could see it from a

hundred yards away, looking me right in the eye. And I felt like it

came to me and wiped away the tears with the feathers at the end

of its pretty wings. I wish it could guide me through this next

step."

"Forever?" Poe asked her.

Then Mary Rogers looked down at the water thoughtfully.

"Should I take a chance on you?" Mary Rogers asked Poe. "You could use a real woman's touch around here. "There is something missing in your life. If you can find it in your heart..."

"I am in no mood to take on another boarder," Poe said. I will bet you would string the boys along and almost take them all the way and then let them down hard."

"I wish I was somebody else," Mary Rogers said. "I wish I had another body."

"Do you believe in telling the truth?" Poe said. Mary Rogers was almost dressed then.

"In a way," Mary Rogers said. "If it works. When you are a kid everybody is trying to change you. And then when you are grown up, nobody cares. Give somebody a year; he will forget your name. I wasted my life."

"When I think about what I was like at your age you scare me to death," Poe said. "I would just drift along and gamble. In the morning I would land in a thunderstorm, hanging on for dear life and just trying to keep breathing. Do you know that feeling? Sliding down with no way to take hold and stop the losing."

"That is when I feel safe and in the arms of someone I love," Mary Rogers said.

But Poe had been operating on distant abstractions all these years. He felt, spinning inside his head a raging murderous fantasy reflecting reproach and cloudiness. He had no place to go. Poe imagined Mary Rogers's body transformed into a fiery spirit. He was not ready to be scorched by her nor was he ready for the madness to stop, nor was he ready to lose her again.

"Can you release me from this chaos?" Mary Rogers said.

"I will try," Poe said. He set his jaw.

Mary Rogers was half-dressed; in a pair of translucent green tights Cinderella might scour the kitchen floor in and nothing else. She was swimming in despair.

"Men can not be trusted," Mary Rogers said.

"I am not like everybody else," Poe said.

"All men judge each other on their own terms," Mary Rogers.

"I can not speak for any other man," Poe said.

"I might like you," Mary Rogers said. "If you put me in a good mood. When you get drunk you say what you really think. I like a happy drunk."

"I am not drunk now," Poe said.

"Climb up here on the roof," Mary Rogers said. She pulled a blouse around her and stepped precariously onto the roof.

Poe stepped onto the roof and sat next to her. The city lights glowed. The moon glowed above the bay.

"You have got to get your feet on the ground. You are in your head too much," Mary Rogers said.

"I am a dreamer," Poe said. "You know that."

"Dreaming about what? Do you ever dream about me?" Mary Rogers said.

"It is my masterpiece," Poe said. "But the heart of the whole plot is still in my head so far. You know who you are; you do not know what you will become. I am not just brooding and hiding out from life."

Poe can see below them in the grainy smoky dark, people's

eyes closed restfully sleeping on pillows in the bland neighborhood. Someone's bedroom window comes alive with the flash of a candle and Poe ducks his head as the woman lights a kerosene reading lamp.

"You should quit drinking hard stuff," Mary Rogers said.

"But still my head is grinding," Poe said. "In my dream last night for instance, I was a new recruit, back at the barracks commander's office. He had a leathery face. Behind him was a map of campaigns. He suspected me of betrayal. Then I stepped out onto a desolate plain, into the shifting sands and I saw you standing at next dune over a thousand yards distant. I shouted, I love you. You said, yes sir. My dream world is as imaginary as this conversation with you, a ghost."

"Who stole my life from me?" Mary Rogers said.

"I can make up a story but that is not the truth," Poe said. Can you tell me what really happened?"

"I am a ghost," Mary Rogers said. "I have a soul. You have a soul. You should leave behind what is dark and vacant.

Find love and respect for yourself. Then you can find the truth about me."

When Poe woke up from his recurring nightmare he crawled out of bed onto the solid wooden floor and walked over to his desk and sat down and took his pen in hand and began writing.

He wondered how he came to this place. He had started, as a poet, he remembered with a rhyme scheme. The force that made him a poet in the first place was real: the ordinary world troubled him, and he tried to make the words work out his troubles. He had been known to invent and re-invent incidents to advance a poem because he was a poet first and reality be damned. But the freedom he had discovered as a poet created problems the form could not contain and he began to transform into a storywriter. But know, he was trying to write a murder mystery. The stark reality of the truth meant he was losing control of the characters he had created.

Poe knew his alter ego, the amateur detective, was both attractive and repulsive to ordinary people. And the real world was constantly in conflict with his imaginary world on paper, where he constructed the text that the characters spoke. Poe knew he had exposed to the public eye his precarious ego, his risky relationships, his dangerous insecurities and it was his struggle to articulate the text that was the problem now. It was the text he had written that controlled the author. He was only a conduit.

The murder of Mary Rogers. Anderson was his patron. Poe had cast himself in many roles, in his fantasies; he had constructed in his mind's eye how he might play the murderer, the dark man. He had even fallen into his brainchild like a cloak every night.

But now it was morning and Poe was sitting here in his glass hothouse garret loft in Manhattan. When Muddie and Sissy woke up it would be a hornet's nest again and tempers would boil like coffee. Now Poe heard groaning conversation from night owls sauntering home and grinding carts and he smelled uplifting smoke. Anderson must have wanted this written as a nostalgic reminder of his employee, Poe thought, but bitter spite often split differences and love simmered at work could bring radical conclusions.

If Anderson approved of Poe's work, Poe could continue writing and he might get a referral for more work. Anderson had read his work. Anderson had liked Poe's poetry because he considered the poems metaphors for Poe's life. Poe laughed to himself, now that the text controlled the author. Anderson preferred a writer like him, who would write a story the way he was told.

Poe wondered how Mary Rogers played her part in this story. She was a character in flux, for certain. Though now that she stood on the other side of the veil, Poe would have to recreate her from his imagination and support his conclusions with evidence. Because she had been murdered, she would never fade far away from his mind, at least until her killer was convicted.

Poe thought there must be three steps in this story, three interwoven themes. The first was distance lends enchantment; the second was the dead are outside the law, and the third was you cannot bury a ghost. Only when those three puzzles were solved could Poe stop the seesaw ride he was on with her ghost. Poe's sense of time had already gone out of joint. He had already been spinning this visionary riddle so long the knots were tangled.

Poe imagined Mary Rogers's ghost waiting up for him, setting him a place, smoking in the nook by the kitchen window, leaning over the wash tub, brushing aside the smoke with a sweeping motion to make it clear away faster, then as the daylight appeared.

I am not some storybook visionary, Poe told himself. Poe had started his first draft last night, imagining Mary Rogers passionately taking on her role when she, who was only a fictional character after all, and so was supposed to be waiting at his beck and call, came back as a ghost. Mary Rogers had now got so out of control that his influence over her characterization became tentative until he could no longer even advance the narrative. But he was ready to start over at the brooder.

This story was a precarious shell that Poe had been constructing in lonely silence. His purpose was to inspire hope. He knew that detachment from history, from other parts of the world and from the past the present and the future, that detachment which engendered nothing but a hopeless feeling about the way things might turn out to be, that detachment was unjustified and unproductive. Since what was and what will be were in flux he would have to find a way to keep them in perspective.

Poe's motives were sublime. What he sought was wisdom, experience and knowledge together with good judgment and understanding. And a reason to keep on living. He was empathetic toward Mary Rogers. He just felt strange writing non-fiction now. He felt more than ever a poet missing a poet's visionary latitude. Writing this true crime murder mystery was Poe's only concrete way of responding to Mary Rogers's still, small voice. He had to laugh at himself for elevating her suffering to his sullen art. But more than the accepted falsehood of fiction, this story was Poe's blueprint for his battle to regain control of his friend Mary Rogers's life and death. Then he might have authority over his own life.

Poe had isolated himself in his little upstairs garret apartment because downstairs his wife and mother-in-law and her boarders had the run of things. Poe's connection to the rest of the world was at stake also, but this connection had been tenuous before. Gambling and drugs had twisted his thinking until he had become grotesque and over-shadowed by morbid fixations. Now all Poe wanted was to become somebody in the real world.

Poe remembered that he had begun rhyming when he was too young to know much, trot to Boston the old trot's dead. As his rhymes became more purposeful, he had discovered the advantages of tinkering with other people's poems. Often poets had a woman in mind, and he had felt a freedom within the confines of his art. A storybook visionary named Publius Ovidius Naso, also known as Ovid, had written Metamorphoses, which reflected the mood swings and transformations Poe was heir to.

These women lost their shame and whored around and white-washed their faces until they were calcified to stone, Poe remembered, So I lived alone and single, working at my art and discovering a creative spirit in myself through my solitary path. I worked through the daylight, sculpting her form, waiting expectantly for my bride to appear in my image, I prepared to make and meet and marry and move in my bride, my still life, no longer still, into our new home, this shrine to her life force, What more high-minded purpose for art could there be than a sculpture

to worship? And what more receptive state of mind than hers?

She will stand as a form for my restless soul, I am hidden away in

the garret of this drab hot-house pursuing my discipline by forming

again her body, I work against the clock in my calm workmanlike

manner with the studied precision of my brush-strokes, Everything

is nearly prepared for the arrival of my bride, Though her

expression is still blunt, her being is becoming real, and though my

dream was once private I am beginning to see her long journey is

nearing arrival, Her face which is not used to conversation is

struggling for form, I mold with my own hands her hands, winding

into woven cords their shape, I work them from a sienna ground

into a color having never felt the sun, I then detail her eyes and

nose and mouth with intricacy staying in harmony with my

medium and my tools and with her being at every step of this

creation, I work against her fleshy surface with my hands, but as

she becomes more real my experience becomes more unreal, I

struggle to shape her form slight in height and virginal and light

weight and I struggle to shape her partially formed body and as I

work her slender muscles, she is delicately hunched over like a dancer with her muscularity lean and yet I hope fertile, I am working my way to her as if this were a long fast with nothing to sustain me but her form and my self now overflowing with passion, There is always strength in simplicity and I know I will someday be able to say it to her that for all these years I have been losing my cleverness and learning how to gain her in spite of my clumsy tools and I will tell her this is an example of God working through the beauty of life, I have been given a unique gift to sculpt her and it is my responsibility to use it, I hope to give her my life, allowing my hand to do what my soul commands, without letting my brain get in the way but both of us living someday in complete harmony, And so God is known by many names: the force of nature, the first cause, light, all beauty and she should reflect that my joy is great just to be loved, This sculpture is an act of worship, in reverent love and allegiance in ceremonies by which love is expressed, with devotion to a sublime spontaneous loving creature of flesh, I struggle against the clock, knowing the essence of my work is its speed and knowing I can only sustain this state of inspiration for a limited space of time and master my energy for a little while to search for my one great love, I was never sure of what I was looking for until I found her within a lump of clay and I discovered I was looking for fulfillment in creating her and so I started over from scratch and let my hand obey the command of my soul and I found that just copying is no art but art is an expression of spiritual existence, But I have also discovered something I could not have expected, and I have fallen in love with my own work, I begin to think she is alive and that is how my art conceals my art, I lift my hand to touch and test out whether she is flesh or clay but I can not admit to myself the truth, I kiss it and I think for a moment I feel my kisses returned, I grasp it and think my fingers press into the flesh when I touch her and I am afraid I have left bruises on her, I speak to it with fondness and love and give it flowers and jewels, I drape it with a beautiful necklace around its beautiful neck, I lay it down on a bed with its head on a pillow and I bend over the couch and kiss her and she seems warm, I kiss her again and touch her breast and the clay grows soft and its hardness vanishes and gives in like wax beneath my fingers as I mold her with my thumb and she become malleable in my grip, I stand up amazed but afraid I am mistaken and doubting what I felt, I try touching her again with my hand and discover she is flesh, her veins are pulsing beneath my fingers, Thank you, I whisper into her ear and I press with my lips her real lips at last, She feels the kisses and looks up and sees the sky and me, her lover at the same time...

So, the rewards of writing poetry had been meager up till this point. As a poet Poe had soon discovered there was little money in poems and nobody wrote them anymore unless they were limericks about Nantucket. But at least now Poe, as a storywriter, had something to fantasize about, a brainchild he could bring back to life, at least in his imagination. And if he also jumped into the mainstream of life, so be it. Why bother to jump in tentatively, step by step. If he could sculpt his brainchild in his mind's eye, she might walk on air, as if on earth.

But then something bizarre began happening to Poe. He discovered the brainchild he had pictured in his mind's eye could not be transfigured because even if his own quid pro quo had turned to stone he was petrified because she was still only made of thin air. And so he took the next step and began working on solving this non-fiction mystery as a way of keeping his feet on the ground.

Consequently, Poe had ultimately found a career as a journeyman editor because poetry would never pay the bills. His mother-in-law still harped at him with tears or silence or winnowed out his faults.

23 POE INTERROGATES SPENCER

THEN POE went to the Tombs to interrogate Spencer. Poe found he had to cajole Spencer's recollection through his laudanum haze.

"We docked the brig Somers near Weehawken Cove, me and Midshipman Rogers," Seaman Philip Spencer said. "We tore down the gangplank," he bragged. Poe saw his stay in the Tombs had not unnerved the young, brash, leathery sailors' cockiness. Spencer had a privateer's bravado, Poe could see. Rogers, Mary's brother, must have been as antagonistic and sneaky as Spencer.

"When we strolled over to John Anderson's Segar Store, Anderson was sitting half-dressed in the back room.

"Will you run get me one pound of foil at Genin, the hatter's, two doors down?" Anderson said to Mary Rogers.

Mary Rogers was sitting in the firelight reflected in the path of spilled aquavit running to an overturned crystal decanter. She whistled as she began to show herself out and unlocking the door, she turned to Anderson, to ask him for money.

Mary Rogers cried out then when she felt her brother's

rough sailor's hands grasp her under the armpits and brusquely lift her up and haul her back indoors.

"Watch your hands!" Mary Rogers called out.

Anderson heard the commotion and was suspicious, so he buttoned his clothes hurriedly. But by then, Mary Rogers had recognized her brother and they were hugging and laughing. Midshipman Rogers was shocked by the change in her form since he left port a year ago.

"From Africa," Midshipman Rogers said awkwardly, holding out his arm. "For you, Mary girl."

Mary Rogers kissed her brother as if she were sucking the life out of his lungs.

"Lubber-boy," Mary Rogers said. "Who is your friend?"

"Spencer, the salty dog," Midshipman Rogers always called me.

"Then I could see Anderson pulling back the drape secretively to have a peek at me," Spencer said.

Seamen Spencer shook Mary Rogers's hand and his rough

grasp lingered.

"Assault and onslaught!" Midshipman Rogers said paternally, stepping in as he pulled their wrists apart. He took his sister in his arms and began dancing with her. He whispered in her ear as they spun. "His father is Secretary of War. His uncle is Judge Ambrose Spencer, who's going to run for mayor of Manhattan."

Anderson overheard some of the words as he eyed them suspiciously from behind the curtain. Spencer saw the curtain flutter. Mary Rogers heard the creaking floorboards as Anderson shifted uneasily in the back of the shop.

"Rescue me," Mary Rogers said to her brother.

Anderson pulled back the drape and entered stiffly smiling at Midshipman Rogers and Seaman Spencer, who sidled to the exit, moving toward Mary Rogers.

"Mr. Anderson, I would like you to meet my brother," Mary Rogers said. She was flustered.

"Midshipman Rogers," he introduced himself, feeling

awkward.

"Seaman Spencer," he said sarcastically, curtly saluting Anderson. "Sir."

"All ashore," Midshipman Rogers said.

"Cease and desist," Anderson said, moving toward Mary Rogers, smiling, gripping her forcefully. Mary Rogers smiled diplomatically to Anderson and lingered, carefully scooting her brother and Spencer to the exit.

Mary Rogers drew Anderson out the door with her and he lingered there.

"He is family," Mary Rogers whispered anxiously.

"Go," Anderson said. "Have a good time." Then he whispered. "Let me know what you find out about Spencer." Mary Rogers looked up into the eyes of her relentless taskmaster.

Mary Rogers and Midshipman Rogers and Seaman Philip Spencer all raced down the street, walking toward a violinist playing a Strauss waltz. Anderson returned to the back room and broke a crystal decanter.

Mary Rogers and Spencer and her brother up to the City Hotel and boarding house where men lounged with their feet hanging out open windows.

Mary Rogers's eyes gazed into Spencer's, yearning to be ransacked.

"Raw and vulgar and common," Mary Rogers said about the lounging men.

Spencer's eyes revealed a sea-wolf's hunger.

"These cynical critics climb out of their cellars to prance around with death," Spencer said about Poe and the newsboys talking on the corner.

Phoebe Rogers was searching anxiously for Mary Rogers and her brother in another part of the promenade, and continued on.

"They just get the public's blood up over outrages, to terrorize the civilized," Mary Rogers said. They passed dandies with bamboo canes. On the river, an iron-hulled steamer moved slowly by, shrouded in mist.

"They play every angle," Spencer said.

"True," Mary Rogers said.

"Or untrue," Spencer said.

Then he pointed out a poster plastered on the brick wall. Grand Vocal Concert by The Rainers, or Tyrolean Minstrels. They could hear a German drinking song with a laughing chorus. Mary Rogers and Spencer and Seaman Rogers went in together. The group was rehearsing.

"Were ever you sea-sick?" Mary Rogers said, fumbling for the words. Spencer grabbed Mary Rogers' arms familiarly, demonstrating his sea-legged motion.

"I learned to hold my own," Spencer said.

Mary Rogers let him rock her, and she was mesmerized.

"Work. Eat. Sleep. Work again," Spencer laughed. "Though I was at the helm of a pirate brig we captured. I love privateering."

The word pirate swept up Mary Rogers.

"Captain MacKenzie says: No survivors. You live three

minutes in that water," Seaman Rogers said bitterly.

"What does your girl look like?" Mary Rogers asked with awe. Midshipman Rogers was pushed out of their conversation by the music. Mary Rogers and Spencer were singing "The Mermaid," as Spencer dressed her in his navy sailor's tie.

"We all just met the eagle," Spencer laughed, paying for their drinks.

Spencer took Mary Rogers into a small dusty shop then, which was infused with smoke. On the floor stood a bucket of water and a sea sponge and her nose rang with the odor of disinfectant and blood. Spencer glanced at the artist's eye. The artist lifted his 3 tightly bundled number 12 sewing needles. Then Spencer ran his finger across drawings of nymphs, distraught Indian maidens, sirens, a circus dancer, a mysterious woman from the East, a star with crescent, a burning heart with a crown of thorns and stopped and then pointed to a drawing of Dürer's four horsemen of the Apocalypse.

A few hours later, in room 3 of the City Hotel, Mary Rogers lazily luxuriated in a serene, private chamber glowing by kerosene lamp. She heard the flapping of wings against the shutter. She realized what they were and then flirted from the shadows into the stark light. She opened the shutter of the window overlooking the bay. A flock of birds rushed away from the window, their shadows crossing hers and vanishing. Church bells started to toll the hour, and the commotion of people walking in the market filled the air. Mary Rogers turned back from the window and her face appeared next to a lily in the full-length mirror riding on hinges. She saw shadows in the mirror rushing past the window and heard the creaking of the stairs as other tenants descended from upstairs. Mary Rogers turned away and sat down by a table with a pitcher of water standing in a bowl. She sang seductively in the mirror, taking out a new silk makeup kit, trying on a new rustling silk nightgown and crossing to the glowing door.

Spencer gazed out over the ships anchored in the bay. His shell was hard. Looking west, across the North River, he saw waving rye fields, slanting trees, blue mountains in the distance, clustering clouds, and heard the sighing winds and the waved slapping the dock. The bell of the Hoboken/Barcalay Street Ferry

clanged 4 times, as it churned toward the Manhattan skyline. It

chugged steam, bucked waves and sprayed, spewing whitecaps. A

buoy's skeletal silhouette, rocked with its eerie, hollow clanging.

The brig Somers's riggings thrashed in the sultry air. The

Hoboken train rushed by groaning trees and whistling, humming

telegraph wires as the engineer signaled one long and one short

wail: t-o-o-t, toot.

Mary Rogers, snug within room 3 of the City Hotel, spun

away from Spencer, shaking her head no, hiding her physical

craving for him.

Spencer felt his hands empty and turned and snuck into a

dark corner and took out his kit-bag and in the shadows he lit an

opium lamp and packed a small pipe constructed of a jointed stalk

of bamboo with a brick of greasy goo. He lit the opium pipe and

then sucked in the smoke and he then snipped the flame out with

his fingers. He waved the serpentine curls of pipe smoke into a

whirl. Spencer saw, as he sunk against the force of gravity

drawing him down against the bed, the room spinning as he disappeared into a cloud of opium smoke.

When Mary Rogers came closer, naively, Spencer placed the stem of the opium pipe in her mouth, but she resisted. He forced the stem in her mouth and covered her nose until she sucked in the smoke.

Mary Rogers's fragile, impressionable eyes were clouded with misty comprehension.

Spencer's dreamy, languid eyes drooped with hooded eyelids. He sat up on the bed languorously and motioned her to him. Spencer and Mary Rogers lay together, serpentine, drowning in smoke. Forgetting their obligations. Light pierced a cracked window glass. Lace curtains slowly brushed apart, driven by breeze off the bay. Light reflected back by a mirror marked by rust. An intimate shadow wedged by a flash of light.

Mary Rogers saw in the rusted mirror, their bodies move in truncated chopped-up slow motion. She continued realizing that it was later now. Spencer and Mary Rogers exhaled opium smoke that clouded the room. Candles fluttered. The room darkened. They gave no indication they knew if it was day or night.

Mary Rogers began running her fingers across the tattoos already drawn on his skin, first the battle royal on his back, an eagle, snake and dragon locked in mortal combat. Then she turned his body over and ran the tips of her fingers across the rock of ages, a woman clinging to a granite cross rising from a stormy sea. She missed the scabs on his arm, and then Mary Rogers ran her fingers down the length of Spencer's body to a rooster tattooed on his right foot.

"Will not fall from the bowsprit," Spencer said.

Mary Rogers then rain her fingers up his leg and around to the tattoo of a rooster on his other foot.

"Will not sink," Spencer said.

"But you fell for me. Say you love me?" Mary Rogers said. She picked up his right hand, which was tattooed with a star and moon. She picked up the other, which showed a small anchor.

"Why?" Spencer asked.

"Love makes the world go around, silly," Mary Rogers said.

"I thought it was the wind," Spencer teased her.

Mary Rogers whispered into his ear.

"Sure," Spencer said.

"Liar, liar, pants on fire," Mary Rogers said, flirtatiously. "If you're too tough then I'll have to love you enough for both of us."

"I thought you belonged to Anderson," Spencer said.

"Mr. Anderson is a perfect gentleman," Mary Rogers said.

"Polite," Spencer said.

Mary Rogers stood up. The chimes in the clock downstairs began to ring.

"I am late," Mary Rogers said. Spencer dressed to go out.

"Where are you going?" Mary Rogers asked him.

"To Washington to see my father, and then I'm bound out for Sierra Leone, North Africa," Spencer said.

"You are dutiful," Mary Rogers said. "All of a sudden."

"I am beholden to my family and the brig Somers,"

Spencer explained, as he packed his gear.

"Spencer? Leave me some," Mary Rogers said to Spencer, stopping his hand from packing the opium gear.

"No," Spencer said.

"I know a secret," Mary Rogers said.

Spencer reconsidered and then gave Mary Rogers some of the opium.

"What do you know?" Spencer said.

"My boss, Anderson, is planning to run for mayor," Mary Rogers said.

"Backed by whom?" Spencer said.

"He is wealthy," Mary Rogers said. "Poe will introduce him to all the newspaper reporters and the magazine editors."

"Introductions and opinions don't buy votes. My uncle's going to own Manhattan, missy," Spencer said.

Spencer gave her his opium gear, and she began humming. She was self-absorbed as Spencer exited.

Anderson was downstairs talking to the front desk clerk of the City Hotel as they looked through the hotel register.

Then Anderson saw Mary Rogers walking downstairs out of the shadows alone.

"Seems plundering doesn't require any letters of marque and reprisal," Midshipman Rogers said. He was face-to-face with his sister. His grip was forceful, her frame was languid, dispirited.

"Hello, sailor," Mary Rogers said, cheerfully but with an eerie hollowness.

"That pirate," Midshipman Rogers said angrily. He recognized her dreamy gaze.

Mary Rogers smiled and pushed him away.

"I am late," Mary Rogers said to her brother. Then she turned to Anderson. "Let's get back to work."

24 MARY ROGERS CHANGED

JOHN ANDERSON'S Segar Store was ringing with the sharp slices of Anderson's knife as he hacked a rolled-up tobacco leaf, dicing it until it was useless. Then he slid the knife across the cutting board with finality.

Mary Rogers had changed. She had a dreamy, distant look. Anderson stood alone and alienated. Mary Rogers could not answer his movements harmoniously, but she seemed pale and melancholy.

"You have been to see your aunt," Anderson, relevant to nothing. He shut the front door and locked it. "I want everything on the table."

"Spencer's uncle is planning to run for mayor," Mary Rogers said.

Anderson did not respond to this old news, but he gazed thoughtfully out the window.

"We don't want to throw around words like love," Mary Rogers said. "I may be a perplexing woman, but I love you with a vengeance."

Anderson watched as a silhouette peered in through the window, and he shut the shutters.

"We have nothing to hide," Mary Rogers said.

"Take the rest of the day off," Anderson said.

Mary Rogers exited then, leaving the door unlocked.

"Unreasonable creature," Anderson said to himself. He opened the casement window, viewing a white sail on the horizon.

Then Midshipman Rogers rushed in brusquely.

"Do you intend to marry my sister?" Midshipman Rogers asked.

"Why should I?" Anderson wanted to know.

"You have used her," Midshipman Rogers said. "I want you to take responsibility for your actions."

"I am above reproach," Anderson said.

"I have heard you own an empty boarding house at Number 126 Nassau Street. If you give my mother the boarding house you own, then I will forget the mistake you made with my sister," Midshipman Rogers said to Anderson. Anderson sat down and wrote out the papers reluctantly and bitterly handed them to Midshipman Rogers.

"This is blackmail," Anderson said.

"Welcome to the family," Midshipman Rogers said.

Anderson locked the door behind him and hung a slate on the knob and scrawled "Closed for Lunch" and left.

At Phoebe Rogers's new boarding house, 126 Nassau Street, Midshipman Rogers and Phoebe Rogers and Mary Rogers proudly unveiled their new home. Midshipman Rogers finished moving in their sparse furniture.

"Do not tell me how you smuggled this," Mary Rogers whispered to her brother.

"Careful navigation," Midshipman Rogers whispered. And then he said aloud for Phoebe Rogers's benefit, "I bought it with the earnings from my voyages. I am shipping out tomorrow, but when I return, I want to see you happy." Then, seeing Mary

Rogers's eye drawn away through the window, "That's all the thanks..." Then Anderson entered, and Midshipman Rogers's expression was dispirited. "... I want."

"I have also set up a country house where we can meet with the thrill of impropriety, but out of the public eye," Anderson whispered to Mary Rogers.

"Some rustic country farmhouse?" Mary Rogers asked.

"Across the North River," Anderson said.

Mary Rogers cried out angrily. "That's good. I was afraid you might want to meet me..." and then flinging back his insult and turning away from him, "...In some out of the way place on some back street." Then she recovered her composure. Anderson superciliously turned his back on her and stormed out the door.

"I am..." Mary Rogers started to say something.

"Better off," Midshipman Rogers said, pouring himself a drink, and overhearing.

Mary Rogers rushed out the door after Anderson, "Sorry."

Mary Rogers followed Anderson to the Arcade Bath, at

number 39 Chambers Street. She slipped into the atrium through the peristyle. She was austerely transformed amid the half-clad men. Her silhouette drew aside the sheer curtain, like a shroud.

"My shadow," Anderson said to Mary Rogers when he recognized her.

"I am quitting the cigar store to live at home," Mary Rogers said, groping for his arm.

"I suppose it was just a matter of time," Anderson said, though he was shaken. He smiled mercurially, and proudly and rigidly recovered his defenses and exited.

Mary Rogers stumbled near the edge of the impluvium. Anderson reached up to seize her. Mary Rogers turned away, embarrassed, moving mechanically to avoid slipping. She started to speak but her voice faltered and she grasped the sheer curtain again, crying into it. Anderson tried to grasp her. She collapsed and he helped her to a marble bench in a tablinum under indirect sunlight. Anderson rummaged through her purse, discovering her opium and her tools.

Mary Rogers restrained Anderson's rage and frustration, by taking his arm as he sat beside her.

"Your habits are shockingly irregular," Anderson said.

"Please," Mary Rogers said.

Anderson helped Mary Rogers lift her groggy form into an omnibus. When they got to Anderson Segar Store, she spilled out of the omnibus. Anderson walked to the door and discovered a red rose Mary Rogers had shoved into the keyhole. On the slate hung for messages, he saw drawn a heart and an arrow piercing it. Mary Rogers tore the slate off the door. Anderson unlocked the door and lay down Mary Rogers on a couch.

While Mary Rogers was passed out on the couch, John Anderson went out looking for Spencer at the docks. He was about to board a steamer for a trip to Washington. Anderson drew him into the shadows.

"I want you to do me a little favor. Kill Midshipman Rogers," Anderson said to Spencer.

"My friend," Spencer said, falsely incredulous.

"In return I will step out of the running for mayor of Manhattan," Anderson said.

"My friend," Spencer said, clasping the back of Anderson's neck.

At John Anderson's Segar Store, Anderson bit a cigar and spit out the plug and carefully lit it 3 times, scorching the surface lightly with flame and then dragging on it until it drew. A whirl of smoke obscured his face.

Mary Rogers heard a creak in the floor, she arose from the couch, but feeling woozy and seeing only a shadow, she sunk back.

"You have changed," Anderson said, moving toward her with menace.

"This is romance, I guess," Mary Rogers said. "I will try to make my feelings match the part you want me to play. You direct me. I have more desire than ever. More yearning."

"Yes, but there are rules just like in any game," Anderson said.

"But I have got to play," Mary Rogers seethed.

"Or you lose," Anderson said.

"You expect me to be an ideal, sexual woman, but it is an ideal I can not live up to," Mary Rogers said, drawing away.

"I wish our nice, quiet paradise could last forever. I have dropped out of the race for mayor, so we can have more time together."

25 POE INTERROGATES ANDERSON

AT NICK Moore's Roadhouse, Poe was drawing Anderson into his interrogation, as they concealed their conversation from the patrons.

"There are a couple of suspects," Poe said.

The moon hovered orange as cirrus clouds raced overhead.

Anderson gazed at the moon morbidly.

"I hope it is another gory one tonight," Anderson said. The waves rippled downstream.

"I remember when we discovered the body," Poe said.

Anderson's composure was cracking)

"This smear campaign drove me out of politics!" Anderson said.

Poe heard the winds howling. Anderson covered his ears. The raw wind railed and shook the hand-blown glass windows. Gray clouds threatened to rain, swelling and swirling. Anderson saw his reflection in the window and pretended to see Mary Rogers standing behind him.

"Where have you been?" Anderson said. He was pretending to see Mary Rogers's ghost. Then he said to Poe, "She says she misses the sun."

Justice Gilbert Merritt then dragged Oscar Loss through the tavern.

"What is the matter with him?" Justice Merritt asked Poe, as he pointed to Anderson. Anderson avoided Poe's gaze.

"I envy your rest," Anderson pretended to be whispering to Mary Rogers. Then he spoke macabrely to Poe. "She says she returns every night to her thicket of thorns to wash her bloody linen."

"He killed Mary Rogers. I know it in my heart of hearts, Poe said to Justice Merritt. Poe was pointing at Anderson.

"I will see her if I have to go to Hell to do it," Anderson said.

"You have got a long ride ahead of you," Poe said to Anderson. The Poe took Merritt aside.

"Truth arises from what seemed irrelevant," Poe explained. "I asked myself what has happened that has never occurred before?"

"It is hard to get the truth from these two," Justice Merritt said, indicating Loss and Anderson.

"Truth is hard to get even from the papers," Poe said. "They parrot gossip. And sensational clichés. I forgot the sensational contradictions and the plain talk taken for profound just because it's to the point. You see, it was misleading. But I want the truth. And in his own way, Anderson confessed the murder of Mary Rogers. Come into the kitchen."

Poe drew the other three into the kitchen. As Poe talked, he took out of the cupboard a meager meal: left-over corn cakes and salt pork and kidney beans and a jar of tomatoes and a sack of flour and a crock of butter and one egg and a box of tea.

"You have changed," Poe coaxed Anderson. Anderson's face became pale and lined, he coughed and moves away, into the shadows in the corner, but Poe pulled him back into the light.

"Eddie's for work. You know," Anderson said to Justice Merritt.

"I am preparing for another bitter lapse into everyday life," Poe said, as he discovered the sugar bowl was full.

Anderson too out five hundred dollars from his wallet.

"Here is your blood money," Anderson said.

"He wants to finance my magazine. And I will take it," Poe said. Poe saw the breadbox was filled to overflowing. He took out a loaf and sliced a piece and buttered it.

"I used to think I was lucky to have him as a friend," Poe said about Anderson to Justice Merritt.

"I have heard about Mary Rogers. The cigar girl," Justice Merritt. "Even here in New Jersey.

Poe took out four plates from the cabinet and laid them out next to the fixings. Then he had an inspiration and began.

"She clung to me," Anderson said.

"And you proposed to free me from my alarm about my future fortune by paying me to solve this mystery," Poe reminded

Anderson. Poe took out the breadcrumbs and breaded the pork and fried it in the skillet and then added tomatoes to the beans and put them into a pot and put on water to boil and reused the last tealeaves.

"But Anderson was bringing news about another kind of undertaking," Anderson said.

26 POE SOLVES THE MYSTERY

"NOW I am going to tell you the solution to this mystery," Poe said. "I have a vague, yet thrilling half-credence in the supernatural. Some of the evidence is coincidence; some comes from a calculus of probabilities. Applying mathematics is an anomaly when its used as the most rigidly exact in science applied to the shadow and spirituality of the most intangible in speculation."

"When I had published *Murder in the Rue Morgue* and *The Gold Bug*, I dismissed the affair and relapsed into my old habit of moody reverie. So, I would work all day and then only go out into public at night. Prone, at all times, to abstraction, I readily fell in with this humor, and continuing to occupy my writing chamber, I gave the future to the winds, and slumbered tranquilly in the present, weaving the dull world around me in dreams. I was credited for my intuition. Here it is."

At John Anderson's Segar Store, at 319 Broadway and Thompson, at 4:15 P.M. on Sunday, July 25, 1841, Mary Rogers ducked down the alley that led to the back door and loading dock

of the store. She saw a shadowy figure walking in the same

direction, a few steps in front of her, but he had not seen her. She

ducked into a shadowy doorway.

"You are still in the race, aren't you?" Mary Rogers

overheard Poe asking Anderson, then.

"I can not afford to run anymore since I have lost the

immortal part of myself, my reputation," Anderson said. As Poe

left, he turned and reflected on the change in Anderson.

Mary Rogers waited until Poe passed around the corner and

then slipped into Anderson's. She carried a paper under her arm.

"Paper-boy," Mary Rogers said. She looked at Anderson's

cluttered workplace with familiarity: she saw a balance book

marked for the business of Anderson's Cigar Shop and another for

Anderson's Solace Tobacco against a stack of unpaid bills and a

chewed pencil and a checkbook gnarled by wear. Mary Rogers

and Anderson approached each other, alienated and distant.

"What kind of world is this? It's out of joint," Anderson

said, turning forcefully. He seized her, but she resisted.

"When your neighbor's house is on fire, it's time to look to your own," Mary Rogers said, regaining her composure.

"Revenge," Anderson muttered, then he transformed in his sternly reproachful side, canceling her gasp with a raised finger. "...Is the perfect hate." And he laughed.

Mary Rogers struck at him and ran out onto the loading dock.

"Do you not know me by now?" Anderson said.

"Stop it. You are scaring me," Mary Rogers said.

Anderson drew her down, and placing his head in her lap, he breathed in her fragrance of cedar smoke and aquavit and Lapsang Souchang tea. Then ruminating, containing his smoldering anger, he said, "Civilization is a thin veneer for rutting animals."

"What is your future?" Mary Rogers asked.

"Am I supposed to read your mind?" Anderson said.

"Yes, you are," Mary Rogers said. "I can read yours."

"Trust me?" Anderson asked. Mary Rogers calculated her strategy.

"If you thirst for existence like me, then you will slake your thirst to drunkenness. What's the matter?" Mary Rogers said.

"Maybe doing the right thing is the beginning of the end for a politician," Anderson said, devilishly. "Your brother is ... "

"True," Mary Rogers said.

"A jolly Rogers," Anderson said. "Listen, honesty is no more than a kind of temporary comfort. I've dredged everything out of myself until life is a series of imitations."

"I believe you are infatuated with the idea of having a child who will look just like you," Anderson said.

"I wake up at night and I feel like I have seen our child," Mary Rogers said. "It is as if he has been in the room with us."

"This is your fantasy," Anderson said. He moved away and looked out the window because he felt crowded. "This is your dream." Anderson was uneasy when she imagined anything.

"You are not helpless and unloved, as you believe,"

Anderson said. "You are mine."

"We have to leave something behind," Mary Rogers said to herself. "Tell me again how much you love me."

"Much," Anderson said.

"I do not want to have your baby," Mary Rogers said. "I do want to have your baby. They are cute, but I just want it to appear like magic."

"I guess having a baby is one step it is hard for a woman to find somebody else to do. Is there somebody else?" Anderson said.

"There is no one else," Mary Rogers said. "It is just having the baby out of wedlock. I want you to marry me because I want you to have this baby with me. You can make it happen. What about names?" She leaned back with her eyes closed to the world. She could feel Anderson's shadow pass over her like a suspicion.

"Why are you so tired? Did you sleep last night?" Anderson said.

Mary exhaled. Then she pinched herself.

"Stitch in my side," Mary Rogers said. "I am going to start showing pretty soon. How are we going to cover it up? Did you hear me? You are not expressing your emotions at all and I am waiting for you to blow up."

Anderson thought, I used to think I was on top of Manhattan. Even Mary Rogers can see I am not fooling anybody. No communication, except all this talk, and that is not even heartfelt. She is collapsing into herself.

Mary Rogers felt she had fallen asleep on her feet. When she opened her eyes, she could not make the words fit together anymore. They were disjointed. She forgets the name of the place names where they were. Long stretches of vapor crossed in the dark where there were no memories to attach her self to.

Mary Rogers had been manipulating her feelings to correspond with the mood demanded of her at the cigar shop. Among those tangled feelings, however, was the feeling that Anderson was using her, and yet she was under pressure from him to act like she was in love. She needed some release, and so, that night, after she and Anderson had closed the shop, and at the time when she customarily walked home, she instead decided to follow Anderson. She enclosed herself in the shadows, expecting that she might follow him home. But he lived north and as she trailed him, she discovered that he walked south. A few blocks from the shop, Anderson entered a secretive place hidden below the street. She followed him in there.

Anderson's body clogged the stoop, his thick fingers rubbing a cloacal old clay pipe. His lips, which were tense at work, had now split into a cherry red maw. His eyes were an artificial red. An acrid organic smoky smell wound up the stairs. Every few seconds the breeze dragged a breath of stale wine up through, too. In the window a trapped wasp framed its inches.

"Good evening," Mary Rogers said. She entered, laughing her husky, hoarse laugh. Anderson, relying on his diplomacy, showed her in the door and gave Mary Rogers a glass of straight whiskey. She saw a dozen people lying on mattresses around the room. Candles flickered over their heads. Young girls brought the sleepy ones more when they wanted more. She sat and the bones of her legs were grinding just under the surface of her red velvet dress. She looked like an ingénue gone to drink, gone to the sway

of the music the violinist played. She laughed again and toasted

Anderson. Her tension twisted, her nerves were stripped bare, her

smile was pinched, her laugh was anxious and breathy, and her

eyes were dazed with sheer need. She was not so much Mary

Rogers that night, as she was raw hunger stripped pale. Her nerves

connected her expressions to her heart. Her face was as white as a

sheet of paper, and on it were drawn her features, though her eyes

were a byzantine labyrinth of expressions. Mary Rogers had

discovered opium and she felt she had cracked a code. Not having

that solution at her fingertips was so horrible that she bit her

tongue when she tried to pronounce the first consonant to

Anderson. Then her eyes, which had always been drawn to

reflective surfaces like lodestone to foil, were lifeless with fantasy.

Where she had usually used any man's eyes as a mirror to monitor

her performance, that night she needed a man only to touch the

opium and then to crystallize something inside of her.

The hunger for opium had become a beast inside of her.

Everything else was out of order. The bitter brownish addictive narcotic drug had slid across Mary Rogers's personality and left behind the thirst for chaos. So there was a jagged grating in her voice, a current of cold air emanating from her as she spoke. She had felt the vicious emptiness of Spencer, his raking, mechanical lovemaking, his whispers rattling up his windpipe. He had murmured his dull come-on, calculated to expose her sense of pride. He faltered from drink, slamming her to the dark with a breath. Mary Rogers found that the untamed instincts he touched were hollow as wind whistling down a stairwell. She sat with a remote air, acknowledging only with a glance the presence of her acquaintances. The opiated air hung around her like a drape, heavy with the incense of this social gathering: marijuana, hashish, Russian cigarettes, the exhalations of the parvenu and opium. She immediately found in her shadowy corner not the expansive but the evasive. She who had been warm outside in the daylight, moist at the hairline, affected a freezing glance that warned many men away. She knew what she was doing. As Mary Rogers watched, with her listless eyes, she became more and more drifty.

She heard an actor lying on a bed in the next room babbling about the way to get in tune with the spheres.

Mary Rogers had wanted very much to be exotic. But the atmosphere in this opium den was one of the inevitability of violence, at least psychic violence.

Anderson coasted through the party with a self-satisfied air, drinking a sherry through a red bent-glass straw.

"I am telling you this in confidence," Anderson said to Mary Rogers. "I have blisters on my throat from inhaling too much opium." He laughed. "I am obsessed with this essential, primal flower."

Mary Rogers was sitting back in a chair, twisting her fingers, picking a speck of opium from her lower lip. She had developed a haunting, faraway gaze. By then it was nearly five a.m. Mary Rogers sat on a bed in the dark shadows broken by a lamp. She pinched her lower lip. She treadled her right leg, brushing leg against leg.

Anderson burst in again, sniffling with an exhaling whistle. Nocturnal, chain-smoker, he fell into an overstuffed Queen Anne wing chair with cabriole legs. His hands lay as embellishments on the chair's arm. His musky air became the same air the room gave off. His mauve Edwardian cut jacket was made to order. His sumptuously flowered shirt was well-tailored privately. She hated him already.

"You are quite the clothes horse," Mary Black said. Anderson nodded and ignored her. There was a hint of lilac in his shirt and the palest regal purple in his jacket. His cuffs brushed Spanish boots. He sat with sureness, lending luster. He French inhaled and the filigree the smoke made as it was sucked into his aquiline nostrils was the same arabesque the pattern of the carpet on the wall made. Absorbed by a winding inner dialogue, he looked as he intended to look when he stood in the wing shadows by the pulleys and the long dangling ropes. His thick and oily eyes intentionally betrayed his restlessness, his petulance. Then, faute de mieux, he took a handkerchief and daubed his nose.

"Listen," Anderson said. "It is my natural indifference that gets me out of bed in the morning, burn my soul. You dimpled harlot."

Mary Rogers slicked her hair back with her thumb and little finger. She took a drag of Anderson's cigarette, and brushed an imaginary ash off the sleeve of her red velour shirt. Her eyes reeled away as she toasted herself, "From obscurity to oblivion."

By then it was nearly sun-up. Mary Rogers and Anderson stood at the window as the party thinned out. Anderson brought out some more opium. A leatherhead strolled by and nodded. The fog was gathering. Mary Rogers was a purely sexual creature when she was taking drugs. It was a sexual rite for her. She would shiver and straighten her spine as she inhaled, in a mixture of raw sexuality and a chilling aphasia. Her hands went limp; her lustrous but morose eyes watched the people moving around her. She tried to disappear into sleep. Anderson cornered Mary Rogers and his expression became intense. He stood over Mary Rogers in a primitive, humanoid, bat like posture, with his arms bent around her.

"You love what I do for you," Anderson said. He shrouded himself in smoke, punctuating each phrase with "you know". He had a boyish roughneck haircut that let the bangs fall into his eyes, but was very short in back. He gestured with karate chops that hacked away at his subject as if it were a lump of plasticene. "I do not need outlet," he said. "People come here to see me. Mary Rogers found herself detesting Anderson and his gang, the disenchanted ghosts hanging around him. Mary Rogers was stunned by how much time they were wasting. "I like your grit," Anderson said. "I like the way you jump out at people from the shadows like a mugger. How would you like to come work for me?" Then Anderson drifted away on a cloud of smoke.

I am living hand to mouth Mary Rogers thought. Inside the den, Mary Rogers was placid and vacant. She fell into suspended animation. She lay back on a leather couch and hours passed like days. But near sun-up she dragged herself to her feet and walked outside. The dawn was noisy. Business had started for the day, and Mary Rogers still wanted to be part of it.

27 PLEASURE RAILWAY

AT COLONEL John Stevens' Elysian Fields resort and the

pleasure railway in Hoboken New Jersey at 4:30 P.M. on Sunday,

July 25, 1841, the air was 89° and muggy. The sun was stark but

the shadows under the poplar and birch trees gave some relief.

The cyclists rode by on the trotting course. A mother lullabied in

Irish as she swung her two children. Another mother whisked a

fan over her infants' face, singing, "Shoo fly." A businessman

showed an architect's rendering of his plans to other businessmen.

Nearby trains whistle wailed one long and one short. The Barclay

Street ferry's deep booming steam hissed as the pilot rang his bell.

At Ludlow's farm, rye harvesters were reaping the field in

the hot sun. Anderson smelled the grain and took Mary Rogers'

hand, pulling her along with the rhythm of the harvesters.

The harvest crew boss drove the crew in a quasi-military

operation. Mary Rogers cowered as the boss's horse stormed by,

narrowly missing trampling her. She flinched at the force and each

of his raspy barks. He returned to driving the harvesters.

"Kill that cock, boy-ohs!" the crew boss shouted. "Storm-clouds rollin' in! Whack it! Whack it!" Then he jumped down from his mount to show them how. "Die! Die! Die!" He crowed. "Kill that cock!" Then he jeered at the laggards. "Come on girls!" He shouted, apprehensively gazing up at the storm clouds. "The little red rooster's going to eat your lunch."

The sweat was streaming and flying off the harvesters, stripped to their waists in the suffocating heat and humidity. Heat lightning crackled against the purple sky near the horizon.

The balers flung rye overhead, ferociously. Finally the last wagon was loaded and they raced for the barn.

"You have done it all, now run for cover!" the crew boss shouted. The crew boss, mounted on horseback, lead the crew on the customary harvest ceremony celebration, driving them to the barn, his face swept alternately with rays of golden sun and furious black shadows. He began singing the song, with musicians both male and female behind him playing and singing along and the crew singing, armed with pitchforks and following and pushing the hay-wagons drawn by oxen. They all rushed the hay to shelter from ruin by the rainwater brought by the impending ferocious storm.

Anderson pulled Mary Rogers along with him into the shadows, racing north under the demonic storm clouds.

In a nearby junction of the lane running north near Sybil's Cave at Castle Point in Hoboken, New Jersey at 7 P.M., visible in the distance was Nick Moore's House, and a disused road. Mary Rogers was shivering despite the heat.

"Is there no place in the world for me?" Mary Rogers said. She lay in the shadows, whispering uneasily, her breath raspy, her dress rustling, and gave out a wispy exhalation. She saw a reeling, eerie view of the leaves overhead. Anderson was braced against her shivering form.

"Have you heard a legend called "The Wild Hunt"?" Anderson said. His eyes were transforming into fury madness. "Some say the wind is a demon dog roaring inside the mountain. Or doomed to hunt forever because he had trampled the crops of the poor." Then Anderson held Mary Rogers's face in his hands. "I know it is the sound of the dead riding back to earth."

Anderson drew Mary Rogers into the thicket, and wheeling around and peering down from the junction of the two roads, he saw on the side of a rough hill, under a sassafras tree, four large stones forming a seat with a back and footstool to it with boughs and briars twined thickly around it.

Next to it, in a hollow, laid a parasol, a petticoat and a scarf and gloves. A white linen handkerchief lay next to tiny high-heeled boots.

John Anderson gazed down at his distorted refection: a puddle of whiskey, a spilled bottle.

Anderson and Mary Rogers sat on the ground, facing away from each other. He was fully dressed, smiling diplomatically. She hummed playfully, but he managed only a wince. She picked up papers that had spilled out of his jacket. She read figures he had jotted down in frustration.

"I saw a castle on our way here," Mary Rogers said.

"That was a monastery. Sanctuary for anyone, as long as you're not a woman. It stands for suffering, you know," Anderson said.

"And hope," Mary Rogers said. "Every night is a pilgrimage of a kind. Even my rough father had faith. That was where he was brave."

"Why don't you write me from the other side when you see him?" Anderson said.

"If you do one thing right, it makes up for a multitude of sins, it can even get you to heaven, my mother always says," Mary Rogers said.

"I was a once a boy in love with being in love, too," Anderson said.

"That is cold sympathy. I am ready to start a new life with you," Mary Rogers said.

"You are living in a dream world," Anderson said.

"When you do not get what you wanted from something, just be glad you did not get what you did not want," Mary Rogers said.

"Does your mother say that too?" Anderson asked. "Be

brave. Say some scripture. Say hello to your brother." Anderson snatched the pages from her tiny hands. He kicked aside their food, smashing the brittle crockery into shards, leaving uneaten corn cakes and pork and beans. Anderson's reflected image splintered in the puddle. Anderson could hear a military band tuning up, and a trumpet soloist started playing, but sputtered to a stop.

Anderson seemed reassured by Mary Rogers's quizzical smile. She glanced up seductively, her lips reaching toward him. Anderson moved his mouth to hers in a kiss. Their eyes seemed to be locked passionately. She opened her lips to his. Mary Rogers looked into his eyes, but his taunt defied her passion for him.

Then Mary Rogers found herself gasping for air. Anderson grasped her around the neck and the ribs and she sunk into his arms. Her cough exploded into his mouth. Blood splattered across his lips and face and ran down his loose shirt. He wrestled her to the rough stone chair. She struggled to breathe. He wrestled her down. He trapped her, cradling her with his arms, but wrenching her neck with his hands. He stormed up onto his feet wildly.

Leaves fluttered overhead as a few drops of rain fell.

After awhile her skin had faded and her eyes were vacant and morbid and pale and her forehead was lined with gritty dirt. She exhaled and shuddered.

Anderson pulled a linen scarf over her face like a shroud. He cradled his skull but lost his footing and turned to look back at her body, rushing away from her.

He slammed his boot into his bottle that splintered.

Anderson looked up toward the sun, which was overshadowed by threatening clouds. The band started to play a military march together. The veterans of the Seminole Indian War in Fort Mellon, Florida were meeting for a reunion. Anderson saw lightning strike a tree then and he heard the band spurt to a stop. A sudden squall blew in from the southwest, blocking the sun. The band rushed to load their instruments in cases. The veterans chivalrously stepped out into the rain and let the flustered mothers and squalling children take cover.

Anderson watched as the storm blew away. Venus was a

fading signal light hanging in the deepening blue. The dark burned away unexpectedly, the sun springing up on the western horizon, throwing a ray across the land, transforming the shades of every dripping object. A cricket creaked. Anderson prowled, looking for witnesses. Mulch sopped, sinking further into the muddy shadows. Anderson flinched at the rumbling in the sky overhead. Anderson watched as the groaning, bruised clouds start roiling in an inverted maelstrom. A hot rain came quivering down in fits and spurts, rattling the trees around. Anderson caught the first few drops of sticky rain on his flesh. The sky above was shagged into jaundiced shingles. He saw a saccharine wreath reading: In Loving Memory. He saw a feminine form appear in a beam of sunlight and wrench into a run and then evaporate. Her words vanished into the damp.

Anderson, as branches, dust and debris clawed his face, cradled his eyes in his elbow. The storm swept in against a towering elm tree illuminated by the snaky lightning. The inky clouds broke into hissing supernatural white veins. Lightning cracked, rain thundered down on the water.

Mary Rogers offered her lips to the storm clouds. She shivered. Her face and the storm breathed together, echoing passion.

Anderson felt the crack of lightning. The rhythm was passionate, intense, and final. The sun sank beneath the storm clouds and the fiery red sun was mirrored in the feverish water.

Mary Rogers lay still. Her breathing had stopped. The crack of lightning and she shivered. In the shady grove the storm and the underlying sunset light flickered through the twisted roots of a thicket. The branches of the tree groaned.

28 HOW ANDERSON KILLED HER

AT THE southern end of Elysian Fields, in the North River near Castle Point, a fisherman and his son who had been fishing from a dory, were struggling to beach their boat and pitch it over on the shore. They rushed for cover, carrying their catch on a stringer northwest toward a tavern shanty. The fountain patrons rushed for cover, leaving one infant behind, squalling. Her mother returned for her, with two other children in hand.

But in the thicket adjoining Ludlow's farm, in Weehawken New Jersey, John Anderson was struggling feverishly to hide his crime. He was becoming more and more aggravated. He ducked into the shadows. Two fishermen rushed by in the downpour, startling Anderson.

When he saw they were gone, he struggled toward their empty dory, lying fifty yards away, pulling Mary Rogers. He had redressed her dead body in her light, striped dress, garters, pantolettes and shoes and roped her into a bundle.

Anderson groaned, dragging her body across rough ground.

He stopped at a sassafras fence-post. He strained to lift a rail and then caught his breath and continued east.

On the West bank of the North River, Anderson strained, lifting Mary Rogers's body and dumping it into a dory. He hoisted the oars up and dropped them down into the oarlocks and shoved off, pulling east 300 yards into the Hudson River. He grunted as he strained to lift her up and over the side of the dory. As he lost his balance, the dory started to pitch over. His hand was caught in her hand, tangled in rope. Her body plunged over the side of the dory, sinking into the river. He jerked out his hand and nursed the rope-burn.

Anderson fell back into the dory, fatigued. Suddenly the sundown was reflected in the river as the clouds began to clear. The sky and its reflection changed cast from pale gray/brown into a firestorm. He jerked his face away from the red light.

Mary Rogers's feminine hand was bound by rope. She seemed caught near the surface, her body floating underwater in the unreal glimmer, light severing the darkness in dribs and drabs. Bubbles rose from her murmuring mouth.

Anderson reached down into the river and pushed her down. She sank into the dark current. She vanished.

Anderson raced to a shady grove in Elysian Fields, which swallowed him. His form flickered through the twisted roots and his feet stumbled on rugged stone. He spun around anxiously. He struggled, slipping into darkness.

In the North River, Mary Rogers's hands were now empty but bound to their mirror image by rope and sinking into the Hudson River. Waves rippled on the shore. The shady trees' leaves sighed. The branches groaned. Manhattan's skyline was visible in the distance. The wet leaves on the oak branches rustled. Sea gulls wheeled overhead, cawing. The full moon and Venus were rising on the horizon, as the sky cleared.

Anderson crouched in the mouth of Sybil's Cave talking to a stalagmite.

"You have been busy," Anderson said. "That's over with. Who's going to know her now?"

29 POE LED ANDERSON TO THE ABBEY

POE LED Anderson to the secluded abbey. As they made their way from the wilderness, out of the shadowy woods, an abbot rang the bell for vespers. Anderson stumbled. Poe knocked at the rusty hinge of the doorknocker at the front gate. The Abbot greeted the bell at the door, dressed in a dark robe with scapular rounded at the bottom and a hood over his cowl.

"Come in, pilgrims," the Abbot said. "Hello."

Anderson wiped his hands on his pants and took the Abbot's arm thankfully and entered.

"We are seeking information about the murder of Mary Rogers," Poe explained.

"We offer refuge and lodging. But no reception for fugitives," the Abbot said pointedly, with a piercing gaze. Anderson winced and adjusted his bearing, offering an innocent demeanor. "We have renounced women."

"This one was rooted out in one generation," Poe said. Anderson confronted his trembling hands and the hid them. As the father lead them across the grounds they were overshadowed by the ruins of a gray stone Gothic church with the roof fallen in and left open to the sky.

"We have renounced women and possessions," the Abbot said. Anderson hid his expression Abbot's glance. Poe could see that Anderson was disturbed and looking up at the bats circling overhead and the ravens chattering. "For sacred peace."

Four lofty arches supported the tower and ivy wound around the pillars in dilapidated fragments choked by brambles. The floor of encaustic tile was spotted with heaps of mutilated sculpture and flat tombstones. The altars were crumbled. The wind whistled through the desolated ruins. The Abbot led Anderson and Poe past the effigy of a knight at the base of a spiral staircase with unsafe and deficient steps. They passed the maimed and dismembered figures of warriors.

The Abbot stooped and washed Anderson's feet. Anderson's face was tormented by grief and humiliation. His face faded to ash. He looked up and saw the deadly pale moon was half-veiled in clouds and heard the wind was gently rustling the ivy over-growing the ruins and the river was lulling near a stone quarry. An owl was shrieking in mysterious echoes. Poe and Anderson left then, as the bells were tolling.

"How shall it be known when a man may in his intercourse with society exhibit everything in a placid manner and yet be possessed of a very violent temper. The one is a result of study and habit; the other is an outburst of nature. The effect of education and polished society is to conceal a harsh temper, yet often when such a man is with those he considers inferiors, the violence embedded in his heart may burst forth in full violence," Poe said to Anderson and the Abbot.

Anderson said nothing.

"Conscience is a verb," Poe said. "An act of conscience is an action your soul takes. That part of you may be visionary, and is part of everything around you for the greater good, or bad, you may not understand what. It is that not understanding."

"I do not believe in wrong-doing," Anderson said. "Why should I feel I was wrong? It is a waste of time."

"You offer a real haven for my crumbling faith," Poe said.

"All I know is that the dead are outside the law," Anderson said.

"Do you believe that specters or spirit are portents returned from the grave by divine permission, or the devil disguised as a dead person?" Poe asked. "What about when peace of mind is lost?"

"I no longer believe in eternal life," Anderson explained. "I do believe in passing on knowledge, in leaving an inheritance."

"I believe in respect for momentary beauty," Poe said. "I wonder about the rest." Poe felt trapped and claustrophobic in this bar. Poe was overwhelmed by an absurdly exaggerated sense of guilt and a morbid fascination with eternal punishment. He bowed in his strange contemplative silence against a tree. Then they continued walking together.

Poe was struggling to control his laudanum addiction, but he took two vials yesterday and today his craving had come on with a vengeance. His lips were parched from wanting more. Poe had always been capable of bluffing. That is what made him powerful at cards. But bluffing him? Had he become so preoccupied with the story of Mary Rogers that he was comfortable staring off into space?

When the sun started going down and the sky began to fade out, Poe was standing near the dueling grounds. He was pausing too long before acting and aiming too low with his ambitions. He had been struggling so hard to bring his future together, that he had blotted out some of his most original thinking.

It was going to be cold tonight. Poe watched the stars and drank in some fresh air. He started tracing the form of the crab and the scorpion.

30 POE AT NICK MOORE'S ROADHOUSE

AT NICK Moore's Roadhouse near Weehawken at 11:50 P.M. on Sunday, July 25, 1841, Poe asked Anderson: "Why did you kill her?" Poe listened for the answer. But all he could hear were leaves rustling against the window, the wind in a long, wispy and melancholy tone, a rasp. Poe rubbed his fingers across his forehead and then gazed up into Anderson's eyes. Anderson evaded Poe's gaze.

"I sought the truth in detail, so I will tell you again in detail," Poe said.

"You derived advantages from Mary Rogers's attendance in your shop," Poe said. "Your liberal proposals were accepted eagerly by Mary Rogers, although somewhat more of hesitation by her mother.

"Your rooms soon became notorious through her charms. She had been working there about a year when she suddenly disappeared from the shop. You were unable to account for her absence. Her mother was distracted by anxiety and terror. The

329

public papers took up investigations and the police were about to begin serious investigations when Mary, in good health, but sad, reappeared at her counter. All inquiry was hushed. You professed ignorance. Mary said she had spent last week with her relations in the country. Then the affair died away and Mary soon quit her job and sought shelter at home with her mother.

"Five months later, she disappeared again.

"3 days passed, and nothing was heard of her.

"On the fourth day, her corpse was found floating near the New Jersey shore.

"The first look we had of her was ghastly. Her forehead and face appeared to have been battered and butchered to a mummy. Her features were scarcely visible; so much violence had been done to her.

"The atrocity of the murder, her youth and beauty and her notoriety produced intense excitement in the minds of New Yorkers. Even politics were forgotten.

"After ten days, a reward was offered.

"The chief of police came to me. The chief was piqued by the failure of his endeavors to ferret out the assassins. His honor was at stake. 'I will make any sacrifice, for your tact,' he said drolly, to me.

"I found out that Mary Rogers had left her mother's house about 9 A.M. in the morning of Sunday, June 22, 1841. 'I am going to see my aunt,' Mary Rogers said. Her aunt lived two miles north, on Jane Street.

"Her fiancé, a drunk, lived at her mother's boardinghouse. He planned to go to her aunt's at dusk and escort her home, but it rained so heavily that afternoon, and because she had before stayed at her aunt when this happened, he chose not to keep his promise.

"As night drew on, Phoebe Rogers said, 'I will never see Mary again.'

"On Monday, Phoebe discovered that Mary Rogers had never made it to Jane Street.

"At noon on Wednesday, June 25, a corpse was towed ashore by some fishermen, who had found it floating in the river.

"Her face was suffused with dark blood, some of which issued from the mouth. No foam was seen as in the case of the merely drowned. There was no discoloration in the cellular tissue. About the throat were bruises and impressions of fingers. The arms were bent over the chest and were rigid. The right hand was clenched. The left was partially open. On the left wrist were two circular excoriations, apparently from a rope. A part of the right wrist was also chafed, as well as the back at the shoulder blades. In bringing the body to shore, the fishermen had attached to it a rope, but this effected none of the excoriations. The flesh of the neck was much swollen. There were no cuts apparent, or bruises that appeared to be the affect of blows. A piece of lace was found tied so tightly around the neck as to be hidden from sight. It was completely buried in the flesh, and was fastened by a knot that lay just under the left ear. This alone would have sufficed to produce death.

"The dress was much torn and disordered. A slip had been torn apart from the bottom hem to the waist, but not torn off. It was wound three times around the waist, and secured by a sort of hitch in the back. The dress beneath the frock was of fine muslin, and from this a slip eighteen inches wide had been torn out very evenly. It was found around her neck, secured by a hard knot. Over this muslin slip the strings of a bonnet were attached by a sailor's slipknot.

"The matter was hushed up by the police. The clothes were identified as those worn by Mary Rogers upon leaving home.

"You were suspected. However, you gave an affidavit, accounting satisfactorily for every hour of the day in question.

"Mrs. Loss said that Mary Rogers came in at 3 P.M. on that Sunday afternoon with a young man of dark complexion.

"An omnibus stage driver, Adam Wall, saw Mary Rogers cross a ferry on the Hudson River that Sunday, with a young man of dark complexion.

"Her fiancé soon killed himself near the location, using laudanum.

"It is the object of a newspaper to create a sensation, to make a point, rather than to find the truth. The masses of people regard as profound only contradictions. Then, just as quickly, the public forgets. So you trumped up some more news.

"Mrs. Loss's boys found Mary Rogers's clothing a full month after her disappearance. You told them to put that false evidence there. You killed Mary Rogers."

"Let me be," Anderson said. His voice was infused with morbid sadness. "I am insane and unable to answer in my own defense."

31 SEAMAN SPENCER KEELHAULED

ON THE outbound brig Somers, the sailors were preparing for a training cruise to Africa, using the square-rigged sailing ship with mainsails fore and aft.

Seaman Spencer was securing the stays on the bowsprit. Midshipman Rogers was at the windlass, preoccupied with securing the hoisting rope around the crank. Spencer clubbed Midshipman Rogers with a rammer for the muzzle-loading cannon, and pushed him over the starboard hand.

Midshipman Rogers plunged into the bay and was keelhauled by the current. An hour later, Seaman Philip Spencer stood, shivering, cuffed and chained in manacles as Captain Alexander MacKenzie read into the wind the charges against Spencer. Spencer smirked in terror. Another shadowy silhouette threw a rope over the yard-arm of the foremast. Spencer's face was cowled over with a hood. The rope was yanked tight around his neck. He was drawn up. Spencer swung out, his feet dangling. The timbers creaked in the spray and the blustering wind.

32 POE FILES HIS STORY

AT THE Snowden's Ladies' Companion, Poe stood, fatigued and hungry. A shadow from a cloud passed by the window. He stepped up to the Columbian iron hand press, and placed a sheet of paper down against the marble slab, which he had already inked. As Poe pulled the bar of the Columbian hand press, a bronzed and gilt machine, its eagle took off, bobbing up and down with every pull of the bar. Shadowing Poe's form, on each pillar of the staple was a caduceus of the universal messenger Hermes and alligators and other draconic serpents at work on the levers. Above Poe's head, the American eagle with extended wings grasped in its talons and Jove's thunderbolts were combined with the olive branch of peace and cornucopia of plenty.

Poe pulled across the hand-grip and the piston rose and he drew out of the hand press the first printed sheet of the story: The Mystery of Mary Rogers, A Sequel to "The Murders in the Rue Morgue," by Edgar A. Poe. Poe held the copy proof in his hand. He could hear 4 bells from the bridge of the steam-driven ferry.

33 POE EARNS THE LUXURY OF SORROW

POE WALKED across the gypsy fortune-teller's tent near Broadway and Old Chatham on Park Row that night. He was drawn in the rhubarb of gypsies outside, when one burst toward Poe, playing a Haydnesque Hungarian rondo on her violin. She was festooned in flashing colored glass and brass. Her dark eyes hypnotically teased Poe.

"I have just published a story," Poe said.

"Your fortune," the gypsy said, drawing him in.

The gypsy lit a smoke for Poe with a spark and lured him into her tent. He could hear the flapping of a raven inside the tent. This sacred chamber was richly furnished, intimate, serene, an enclosed garden of sighing wind and stars. Poe heard the flapping wings again and he could make out in the shadows, an ebony raven appearing and lighting on an ancient bust. The nonchalant gypsy, her sad eyes ominous, read Poe's tarot cards.

"This is the hanged man," the gypsy said, embracing him playfully. The gypsy showed him a card. Poe could see himself on the card. The blue figure of Poe hung upside down with his legs crossed. Poe sprung free of her grasp.

"His mask is in flux and there is a cell beyond him. A secret riddle?" the gypsy asked. She covered his face with her fingers.

"Where is she?" Poe asked.

"She comes and goes," the gypsy said, as her as her right hand formed a "C" and her left hand formed a "C" and she placed them together and then let her hands fall.

"Like the moon," Poe said.

"She may be a seed. The stars grow gray in giving birth and death," the gypsy said.

"Human kindness is overflowing," Poe said to the raven. The raven dropped dead. Poe recoiled recoils, stunned. He looked over to the gypsy, who appeared overwhelmed with grief. Poe then reached toward the raven instinctively. The raven came back to life and flew away, cawing. Poe and the gypsy then backed away from each other, the gypsy laughing cynically. The raven soared, emerging and then disappearing in shafts of light within the gridiron structure of the square, then winging back to her. The gypsy laughed, her jewelry jingling. Poe looked up and saw the sun glowing through a spider's wet web. He heard church bells echoing. He heard foghorns echoing, fading.

"I always have the luxury of sorrow," Poe said. He sipped from his vial of laudanum and his eyes sunk from constriction into dreamy somnambulism.

33 A CUP OF CONSOLATION

AT ANDERSON'S home in Tarrytown that night, Anderson buttoned his black beaver-cloth overcoat with velvet lapels and closed his steel shutters.

In the smoky interior of the Sign of the Crow Tavern that night, crowded with sailors and racetrack touts and gamblers and con men and prostitutes and showgirls, Poe placed an order at the bar.

"A cup of consolation," Poe said. He inhaled the fragrant scent of other people, and drank a chartreuse-colored liquid laced with opium, falling into a dream.

Poe dreamed of Mary Rogers, her body spinning down the slowly whirling river. She was mischievously and enigmatically smiling. The river lifted her and the strands of her hair interwove like waves. Her image was infused with the moist inhalations of hookah-like breathing, which blended with a melancholy tune played on a sheng, a raspy Chinese mouth organ.

"Eddie?" Mary Rogers called.

Poe dove in after her, his desire and his morbid passion driving him to strip off his clothes underwater.

Mary Rogers's shining, living essence swam through the water's shadows, and the two of them surfaced together, but then she rose into the mist. Poe lay, floating in the water for a long time.

<<< The End >>>

List of Sources

New York Public Library, New York City.

Pierpont Morgan Library, New York City.

Thomas, Dwight, and David K. Jackson. *The Poe Log, A Documentary Life of Edgar Allan Poe, 1809-1849.* Boston: G.K. Hall & Co., 1987. Print.

Quinn, Patrick. *Edgar Allan Poe, Poetry and Tales.* New York: The Library of America, 1984. Print.

Peithman, Stephen. *The Annotated Tales of Edgar Allan Poe.* New York: Doubleday, 1981. Print.

Markham, Edwin. *The Works of Edgar Allan Poe.* New York: Funk & Wagnalls, 1904. Print.

Walsh, John. *Poe the Detective: The Curious Circumstances Behind the Mystery of Marie Rogêt.* New Brunswick, New Jersey: Rutgers University Press. 1967.

Hammer, Rick. *This Mortal Tale.* New York: New York Press. 1988.

Poe's signature for the University of Virginia, public domain, common property. Commins.wikimedia.org/wiki/file:Edgar_Allan_Poe_signaturesvg.

Illustration by Tom Chalkley.

ABOUT THE AUTHOR

Rick Hammer lives in Tulsa, Oklahoma with Brit, his wife for thirty-three and a third years.

Made in the USA
Charleston, SC
22 October 2015